An *Ó Seanacháin* Publication

Editorial Production: Marc Shanahan
Graphic Production: Gabriel Shanahan

I.

Introduction

Tribal societies often have ceremonies by which they initiate young people into adulthood. In America, there are few moments that mark the transition from youth into adulthood: the age of legal driving is one of them.

I approached my sixteenth birthday with the same anticipation we all did in those days. My birthday fell on a Friday that year, and my father had promised he would take me to the DMV office for my driver's test. At school, I could barely control my glee.

Then, midway through third period, the school intercom crackled and the principal's voice came across filled with tense uncertainty: "We've just heard a radio bulletin that shots were fired at President Kennedy's motorcade in Dallas. The president has been taken to the hospital, but there's no word on whether he was hit . . . we'll keep you posted on further announcements."

After a moment of silence, the room began to buzz. The first distinguishable remark I remember hearing was one of the class cynics saying, "Hell, it's no big deal. They probably just shot him in the hand or something. He'll live." But just before the class ended, the intercom crackled again and the principal announced that Kennedy was in critical condition with massive head wounds. The bell rang as he finished speaking, and I headed for an algebra test filled with confusion.

The morning sky darkened with the threat of rain. About fifteen minutes into the exam, the intercom crackled one last time and the principal announced that the president had died at 1 PM, Central Standard Time. There were murmurs in the room, and one barely audible curse aimed at the teacher who had insisted on us taking the exam as scheduled.

Throughout the rest of the school day, I remained deeply troubled, not only by the assassination but by the torment I felt: part of me was set on taking the driver's test that day at any cost; another part of me thought that an embarrassingly selfish thing to do.

When my father picked me up around three, he asked if I still wanted to go to the DMV offices. Trying to feign nonchalance, I suggested that we drive by to see if the offices were still open. They were, and within an hour I had passed the test and received my license.

When we arrived home, my mother and a friend named Betty were having coffee. Betty handed me a small wrapped gift and said, "Happy Birthday . . . for what it's worth."

I went to my room and sat looking out the window at the family car, which sat in the driveway, mine to use now if I wanted. But the thought of going for a drive left me cold. As the light in the room faded, I noticed a stack of newspapers on my bookshelf, front pages that I had saved from important events – Alan Shepard's flight, Kennedy's election. I realized that the evening paper would go on that stack, and with it would go the possessive feeling that I had always had about November 22. My next birthday would be the first anniversary of JKF's death. When I turned 21 it would be the fifth anniversary. I thought of Betty's remark and how I had been hurt by it. But I realized she wasn't to blame: the president was dead. It was a terrible day.

I walked down the hall toward the living room to watch the television reports with the rest of my family. Somewhere along the way I forgot completely that it was my birthday.[1]

---

[1] Taken from "Transitions" by Dan Shanahan; *The San Francisco Sunday Examiner & Chronicle*, November 20, 1983.

If you were, say, seven years old or more on the day of JFK's assassination, and American – though not exclusively – you almost certainly know where you were when you heard the news. Because the world changed that day, forever.[2]

It is hard to explain to those born after 1960 or so what the world had been like in the years preceding Kennedy's assassination. After the end of World War II, Middle America was free to pursue the American Dream without the hindrances they had experienced up until then: the haunting years of the Great Depression, the brave but burdensome years of the war. The Fifties were the quintessential "good times" everyone hoped for during the first half of the 20th century, and they were marked by a calm and a sense of entitlement – that the new era had been both earned and "won" by those of Kennedy's generation – that underscored the great promise that lay ahead for the country.

---

[2] I'm aware that there are those who feel that the 9/11 attacks were of a kind as significant – perhaps even more so – than JFK's assassination. On a number of counts – most especially that Dallas came when the country was still in its post-war prime, that it radically altered the course of national policy for decades to come, and that it had its origin *inside* the country rather than from outside – I continue to consider the events in Dealey Plaza more pivotal. But it's entirely possible that the overreaction to 9/11 – most especially in the catastrophically ill-advised military responses it produced – could eventually prove to be equally devastating to the fabric of 20th century American history.

Moreover, by the end of the Eisenhower presidency – a time during which people had basked in their achievements – a new spirit was beginning to emerge. It could be felt in the music, in cinema, in journalism and literature: it was that feeling that comes when, after a well-earned rest, resting threatens to become boring and we want to get back to work.

But no one knew what that work should be, and JFK – his youth and energy a decided contrast to Eisenhower's grandfatherly presence – became emblematic of the appetite to embark on some new journey, to take on some new challenge, to conquer some new . . . frontier. I well remember a picture in *Life* magazine during the summer campaign of 1960 leading up to the August conventions, a shot of a crowd awaiting the just-landed senator from Massachusetts at some small, Midwestern airport, half a dozen young-ish women holding up a sign they had fashioned on a bed sheet. It read:

Start packing, Mamie: Here come the KENNEDYS!!!

It was an emblem of the times: self-confident, iconoclastic – *young* – and full of spunk, ready to take on the world. And it caught fire. I remember JFK announcing that 50-mile hikes would be required of all military personnel to prove their combat readiness, and the entire country took on the challenge, so much so that

warnings had to be issued that undertaking a 50-mile hike might

actually be harmful for those unprepared for its rigors. There was

something afoot here, and it wasn't just walking. There was, indeed,

a hunger for new challenges in a population that felt it had

successfully defeated the monster of economic depression and the

dogs of war, and Kennedy seemed to embody both the spirit of those

successes and the hunger to achieve more. Psychologists and

political scientists will argue for decades to come whether or not, or

at least how much, JFK deserved credit for that spirit and how much

the country's aspirations were projected onto him. Both were clearly

true, and, whichever the way the balance tipped – towards true

leadership, or joyful delusion – the entire "thousand days" of the

Kennedy administration were energized by the new spirit JFK called

the "New Frontier."

But that fortuitous intersection of leadership capability and

the desire for new directions not only led to the enthusiasm which so

characterized those thousand days[3], it immeasurably amplified the

---

[3] It has been said that it was Jacqueline Kennedy who cultivated the Camelot view
of the Kennedy years, and in fact that view is more an after-the-fact impression. If
one were to look for a musical from the time that evoked the excitement and the

magnitude of the horror experienced when they were brought to a brutal halt on the streets of Dallas. The searing of the American consciousness by the events of that November were not simply the result of the loss of a popular – for many, but not all[4] – president, but the consequence of an end that was virtually the antithesis of what had gone before. It was as though anti-matter had destroyed matter, darkness commensurate with the prevailing light had descended upon the national soul – almost as though the enthusiasm and excitement had itself provoked some kind of vengeful dark evil as a response. People have tried to compare this episode in American life to Greek or Shakespearean tragedy, but the better comparison might be to America's own *Moby-Dick* – albeit substituting a young enlightened captain for the mad Captain Ahab, and an almost cruise ship atmosphere for that of the doomed Pequod in the lead-up to the cataclysmic denouement.

Nor can it be denied that the Warren Report, even when it first appeared, did much more than provide a hollow coda to the

---

verve, it would more likely be something like "Bye Bye Birdie."

[4] Walter Brennan, beloved by Americans of that time for his portrayal of Grandpa McCoy on the popular television show, "The Real McCoys," was said to have done a jig on the set at the news of JFK's death.

cataclysm. The notion that an improbable sequence of events – the antiquated rifle, the inhuman accuracy, the "lone nut" behind it all – could have brought an end to so euphoric a time in the life of a people rang false. Norman Mailer would one day try to portray the nagging unwillingness of the American public to accept the improbable official explanations as a kind of nostalgic disbelief that life could be so cruel, a desire to find causes fittingly commensurate with what was lost, no matter how delusional the causal explanations might be. (He ignored the fact that the single assassin theory works the same logic in reverse: allowing one to escape the possibility that dark, complex forces undermining democracy might have been at work.)

But Mailer, and the Warren Report, were both wrong – and monumentally condescending.

Mailer failed to appreciate the extent to which the American people often, if not always, intuit the truth and respond to it. The outpouring of sympathy for the Civil Rights movement after the dog attacks of the first march across the Edmund Pettus Bridge in Selma; the outrage felt after the police attacks on demonstrators at the Democratic National Convention in Chicago in 1968; the growing discontent with the falsehoods pandered about by the federal government during the Vietnam War; rejection of Richard Nixon as the Watergate revelations unfolded – these are only the highlights of the moments when the American public has been able (sometimes only after much reluctance, it's true) to see through the fog of the official narrative to the real truth.

Thus it has been that Americans have, over the course of the more than half century since Dallas, felt growing – and finally utter – dissatisfaction with the official version of what happened there and have shown, especially in the guise of a few dedicated researchers, mostly independent and largely unaided by establishment historians, a determination to, as the saying goes, "get to the bottom of this." My first engagement with the notion that the Warren Commission report might have been fraught with contradictions came with the David Lifton exposé that appeared in *Ramparts* magazine in January of 1967. Soon after, I enrolled in the San Francisco State Experimental College course on the assassination and within weeks was privy to requests made by the District Attorney of New Orleans to the course organizer for any information any of us might have about the visits of a "Clay Shaw" or Clay Bertrand" to San Francisco in 1963. At night, after class, I went to the Greyhound bus depot just off Market Street where the New Orleans *Times-Picyune*, with its detailed account of the Garrison investigation, could be found.

I followed the early books: Mark Lane's *Rush to Judgement*, the *Whitewash* volumes of Harold Weisberg, Richard Popkin's *The Second Oswald* (on which I wrote my paper), and others. But as the years dragged on, and particularly after the feeding frenzy the press engaged in as the Garrison investigation was sabotaged, I drew back. The HSCA hearings gave me some hope, quickly dashed, that the truth might be exposed and validated by the press; I simply sampled things from time to time after that.

But the die-hard investigators soldiered on, despite the fact that they were bullied by the press from the very beginning. Lifton's 1982 *Best Evidence*, its painstaking review of the twists and turns in the official version of the Bethesda autopsy report justifiably nominated for a Pulitzer prize, should have established the credentials of the research community once and for all; but it did not. In fact, one wonders what might have happened if Oliver Stone had not adopted the Garrison story and made *JFK*. A cinematic tour-de-force that laid out what Garrison had uncovered without the sniping and scoffing that the investigation had encountered a quarter of a century before, it awakened the skepticism in the American people and provoked sentiment that led to the formation by Congress of the Assassination Records Review Board. That body, though its brief was merely to uncover and archive evidence that might be relevant to the assassination, made available a wealth of material to researchers who sifted through it with all the care it required.

It hasn't always been pretty. Anyone who has followed the growth, since the rise of the Internet, of assassination chat rooms and dedicated Face Book pages, has seen the extent to which some disbelievers in the Warren Commission have been intolerant, self-important and downright vicious in dealing with even those who agree with them that the official narrative is bogus, but who may differ on the specifics of what actually took place in Dallas. But much more good than bad has come of what has become known as the community of "conspiracy theorists" – a term which, itself, smacks of some of the dismissive caricatures of researchers drawn by the media.

The early books exposing the huge holes in the Warren Report; the work of some, like Gaeton Fonzi, who worked with the

House Select Committee on Assassinations to begin to uncover hidden pieces of the puzzle of what really happened; the subsequent truly ground-breaking empirical studies of crime scene and medical evidence done by David Lifton, Douglas Horne and Sherry Feister; and the game-changing revelations of Judith Vary Baker – each in its own way has, along with the work of others and the avid support of readers eager to uncover the truth, brought the investigation of the Kennedy assassination to the brink of a new era, which this short summary discussion is itself about.

But though there is a wealth of information still to be discovered about the assassination, how it came about, how it was executed and how it was covered up, assassination research too often risks descending into petty bickering about minutiae. People with strong feelings about, say, the involvement of Lyndon Johnson in the conspiracy may, for instance, fixate on whether the open rear driver's side door on the car in which Johnson's security detail rode, indicates a signal to the vice-president – even though having a door open when the security detail was not, as was the case with JFK's detail that day, in an open car, was standard Secret Service procedure. Others may dwell on the number of shooters, the number of teams, their location and/or their identities (not inconsequential matters). Thanks to a back injury I suffered on a trampoline about ten days before JFK's election, and which injured a vertebra at about the same level as the holes in JFK's jacket and shirt suggest he was shot, I have always been unsatisfied with the description of the president's first reaction to being shot described as "reaching for his throat": as a fellow sufferer, I feel strongly that he was reacting to being struck violently in the back.[5]

All too often, disagreements about these matters descend into scoffs, derision – and worse – when the real import of the discussion should revolve around how a specific detail, large or small, fits into the larger picture *that must be out there* just as surely as the details of making the cup of coffee that now sits on my desk are. What those of us who want to assemble a viable version of what really happened must do is *accept that we are all in search of that version and work together to assemble it on the basis of our common ground.* But part of the difficulty lies in the fact that we need to have at least an outline of what likely transpired against which to test

---

[5] Move both your hands towards your throat from a resting position: your elbows do not fly out and up as JFK's obviously did.

all our hypotheses and disagreements, and to update that outline regularly and, as much as possible, by common consent, as new evidence and/or conclusions become available. And, right now, we only have the thinnest of probable scenarios. They usually come at the end of a long examination of the evidence, much of the discussion devoted to refuting the Warren findings, the "lone nut" believers, the scoffers and the patent obfuscators. Not an environment that is likely to make developing consensus an easy task.

However, I think we can be encouraged by the quality of the best work that has been done over these more than five decades. That work demonstrates that determined researchers can make progress, despite the internecine strife that may erupt, and the historical record be put straight, slowly but surely. And that fact – and especially the sense that we are on the verge of a new stage in our overall knowledge – is what lies behind this attempt.

It's early, to be sure. Some researchers will rightly scoff at developing anything like a detailed overview, given the limits that necessarily exist at this stage of the game. And there will be those who are eager to put down the attempt, and its author, out of conviction that they have the real answers to the questions, the real solution to the puzzle. Fine. For if this effort serves as nothing more than a target for shooting practice, a punching bag or a straw man, it will hopefully turn the attention of some to the next real task at hand: painting a portrait, in as much detail as possible, of *what actually happened* in its entirety, from Lee Oswald's Marine service through the countless improbable deaths of witnesses and others involved in the assassination and its aftermath.

There may be those – largely outside the research community – who would ask "why bother?" In one respect, I think that question underlies some of the conflict that one sees on such things as Face Book discussions of the assassination. (I speak here of the internecine strife among disbelievers in the official version, not between the Warren Report defenders and their opponents.) For, indeed, there is no chance of legal justice "being done" in the case of the Kennedy assassination. There may be a few survivors of the plot to kill JFK lingering in advanced old age here and there, but it is almost certain that those most likely responsible for putting things in motion and monitoring the plot's progress – the Allen Dulleses, David Attlee Phillipses, and Carlos Marcellos – are in their graves, beyond the reach of the law. Some of the shooters may still be around, but they were, in the end, rather minor players in the larger crime that was committed in Dealey Plaza that day. But that's where the passion of the researchers comes in.

People who want to know the truth about the Kennedy assassination want, first and foremost, to know *the truth*. Secondly, they want to know what was done to their country by the conspirators and the plotters – for them, exposing the truth represents some kind of justice. But a third, and perhaps most important motive lies in the fact that history is at stake – and history is the story of who we are. Few people know that, when the Japanese cabinet replied to the American demand for surrender shortly before the dropping of the atomic weapons on Hiroshima and Nagasaki, the Japanese new agency Domei mistranslated one of the words in the cabinet's message as "ignore" [the demand] rather than "withhold comment [on the demand] pending decision." The cabinet was seriously considering accepting the American terms; the Americans were (wrongly) told their demand was being ignored. As a consequence, the first use of thermonuclear weapons in human history went ahead and hundreds of thousands of lives were lost.

Though Domei's catastrophic language miscue is well known among historians of that episode, it is not largely known in the world at large. It should be. There is no blame to attach, no undoing what has been done. But the knowledge of how often countless lives can hang by a thread would make for a much more sober view of war and peace in our world.[6]

So, too with the assassination of John Kennedy. The most likely explanation for JFK's assassination is that forces, both within the government and without, coalesced to eliminate the president because of the policies he had pursued during his thousand days in office. More will be said about those below. But it must become part of the historical record that the elimination of a sitting president was possible and did take place if we are to truly understand our history. That realization will, no doubt, shake the American body politic to its foundations – indeed, it has taken less to bring political

---

[6] Ironically, an intentional misinterpretation of sorts took place during the Cuban Crisis, when JFK chose to ignore a more adversarial reply (obviously written by the hawks on the Politburo) Khrushchev had sent to Kennedy and answer a first, more conciliatory note that it was felt represented Khrushchev's true feelings. Countless lives may well have been saved by that stratagem. One wonders how many times in subsequent years such deft diplomacy might have kept us from the seemingly interminable and bungling foreign involvements in war that became almost the norm after Kennedy died. See Dallek, *John F. Kennedy: An Unfinished Life* (London: Allen Lane, 2003); Chapter 16.

regimes down through history to their knees. And I think there have been those involved, if only by their silence, in covering up the truth about the assassination because they feared the Republic might not survive full disclosure of what took place.[7] I have no reason to disagree with that assessment.

However, I have no concern that such a collapse of confidence in government is at risk from researchers' work today. For one thing, a majority of the American people already believe JFK *was* killed by a conspiratorial group, and this has no doubt contributed much to the anger and cynicism about government that exists today. More importantly, I don't expect any "smoking guns" to emerge in my lifetime.[8] What is more likely – and more necessary – is that the slow, hard, painstaking work of researching, probing, and hypothesizing with judiciousness and care will ultimately draw out the larger truth, both in its nuances and its overarching implications, and that history will eventually be put right. When the critical mass is reached in drawing out that truth,

---

[7] I include members of the Kennedy family, RFK among them, as likely to have had this attitude and kept what they doubted and what they knew to themselves for that reason.

[8] There are documents still to be released in a time frame that might allow me to be around when they are. I have my fingers crossed.

the American people will have the task of facing it as judiciously and as determinedly as those who have assembled it have been. It will no doubt be a process that will itself take time.

II

The Setting

Any serious attempt to come to terms with what really happened in Dealey Plaza must start with a look at the backdrop against which the events that November took place. Many studies do that,[9] and though some of the material contained herein may be repetitive, recounting it, at least in brief, is essential.

Though it's rarely looked at this way, it's safe to say that when the Kennedy brothers came to town in 1961,[10] they saw themselves to some extent as the good marshals come to clean up Washington. High on their list were "the mob," as it was called, and

---

[9] Douglass' *JFK and the Unspeakable*, (Maryknoll: Orbis, 2008), though marred by being thoroughly hagiographic, is one; vol. 5 of Douglas Horne's study is another.

[10] Though JFK was clearly the holder of power, the chemistry between he and his brother, as well as the "clan" style of the family, make it worthwhile to think of the two as a team. The fact that the dying Santos Trafficante said "We should have killed Bobby" and that RFK ultimately did meet his brother's fate, underscores the dyad they represented.

Fidel Castro. RFK carried the ball on both these "missions",

bringing to them the same, sometimes misplaced zeal – and even

bravado – that he'd brought to his rather virulent work as a staff

member for the Senate Labor Rackets committee. But JFK was fully

apprised of what his brother did and supported him in most matters.

In the early days, however, the brothers were probably

hamstrung – and considerably so – by their father's ties with

business and even the underworld and by the pressure those ties

brought to bear on what they felt free to do – not to mention the very

strong personal influence an Irish father was likely to have on the

sons whom he had pushed into public life and helped immeasurably

in their successes. Thurston Clarke has underscored the fact that

Joseph Kennedy's stroke in late 1961, and the severe disabilities –

especially aphasia – that resulted, most likely left him so debilitated

that his sons finally felt free to be their own men and to act in the

fashion they saw fit. The strong opposition mounted by the

administration in the face of substantial steel price hikes – a

throwing down of the gauntlet often compared to FDR's many face-

offs with big industry and Teddy Roosevelt's challenge to the power

of the monopolies – which included investigations of corporate officers by the Justice Department, made clear that the brothers were not going to sit by and be bullied by big money; they themselves were monied, they could play hardball. That attitude would lurk just beneath the surface during the subsequent year and a half of the administration, best characterized by JFK's remark, "My father always told me that all businessmen were sons of bitches, but I never believed it until now."

But perhaps the most important part of the backdrop to the events that would take place nineteen months later were the clear signals that came early and continued with increasing force in foreign policy. JFK's refusal to provide the air support which he had been told would *not* be needed for the Bay of Pigs debacle – itself the child of the Eisenhower administration, and especially Richard Nixon – was probably the largest domino to fall in the sequence of events that led from Inauguration Day to Dealey plaza, for it allowed the most rabid members of the anti-Castro movement to ignore or dismiss the Kennedy brothers' strong stance against Cuban communism and to perpetuate the same "stab in the back" myth that Hitler had used to come to power in Germany in the Thirties.

The utter failure of the CIA to provide realistic assessments –

in fact, its willingness to blatantly cherry-pick and even to attempt to

corner the President into taking unwise action – before and during

the fiasco also led JFK to detest the Agency, to recognize, as Truman

had, belatedly, that the intelligence "community" was a Frankenstein

that had to be dismembered. The President started to do so by firing

its high chief, the equivalent of J. Edgar Hoover in the FBI, Allen

Dulles, Deputy Director Charles Cabell – whose brother, Earl, would

be mayor of Dallas when the assassination took place – and another

Deputy Director, Richard Bissell. JFK was quoted as telling a friend

he wanted "to splinter the CIA into a thousand pieces and scatter it to

the winds."[11]

But at the same time, the humiliation suffered by the brothers

in the first face-off with one of their arch-enemies, Fidel Castro, led

them to redouble their efforts to bring the Cuban leader down.

Bobby especially seems to have developed an almost obsessive

preoccupation with insurgency against Castro and plots to

assassinate him, and this gave rise to Operation Mongoose, a covert,

_____

[11] http://www.nbcnews.com/news/other/inside-job-cia-suspect-some-jfks-killing-f2D11627219

CIA-led operation to bring Castro down and over which RFK retained control – even in the face of an attempt by the Military Joint Chiefs of Staff, who were also considered by JFK and RFK to have shared culpability in the Bay of Pigs debacle, to put the operation under their own control. Mongoose, and especially the JM/WAVE station established in Florida by the CIA for support activities, arguably functioned as a toxic stew out of which everything from plans to invade the island to foot soldiers and weapons used in the failed attempts to assassinate Castro and, finally, the successful assassination of JFK emerged.

And if the Bay of Pigs fiasco can be seen as the first and largest of the dominoes to fall on the path to Dealey Plaza, the Cuban Missile Crisis can be seen as the turning point which made that path inevitable. For, in the face of intense pressure from all directions – the anti-Castro Cubans, the intelligence agencies and the US military (especially, and virulently, in the person of Curtis LeMay) – the brothers stood fast and, as the records clearly show, picked their way through the world's first, true nuclear minefield to a negotiated diplomatic settlement (albeit with some military muscle-flexing) that pulled the superpowers back from a conflict that could quite clearly have transported much of humanity back to the Stone Age.[12] Moreover, it's quite clear that the clean-up-the-town bravado and missionary zeal of both brothers was vastly tempered by the experience of a true nuclear confrontation.[13] JFK "established a connection" with Khrushchev we might say today – something that would have been unthinkable only a year before – and the fruit of that connection and the sobering experience that brought it on no doubt lay behind the president's famed American University speech on disarmament and world peace. That, combined with the deepening conviction among the anti-Castro forces, the military and the intelligence community that Kennedy was permanently "soft on communism" and thus a danger to "the American way of life", probably sealed his fate, if it had not been sealed already.[14]

There need only be added a bit of micro-motivational background to complete the picture, for without a doubt one of the greatest obstacles to creating an accurate portrait of the background

---

[12] In this regard, there is still no better portrait of how life might have unfolded after a nuclear war than Pat Frank's 1959 novel, *Alas, Babylon*.

[13] As was that of the American public, as I've argued in "The Cuban Missile Crisis: Memoirs of a Survivor," in Vito Perrone, *Visions of Peace* (Grand Forks: *North Dakota Quarterly* Press, 1988).

[14] Ironically, Castro's own caution came at the price of losing his most valued comrade, Che Guevara, who wanted to take command of the Soviet weapons during the crisis and use them.

to a professional murder is the "it can't happen here" reflex most Americans share, perhaps better characterized in the case of JFK's assassination as "how could this possibly happen here?"

I'll be the first to admit that the progress of my attitudes towards the official explanation of the assassination followed closely my awakening from a comfortable-but-complacent attitude towards "the American way of life" of the 50s and the birth of skepticism about "the Establishment" that took place as I grew older. Vietnam, Civil Rights, the excesses of the Johnson administration in response to legitimate protests against the war, and, later and even more darkly, the ghastly defiance of principles of American democracy by the Nixon administration in so many areas – all these contributed to my willingness to challenge the official explanation, whatever it might be, until I was satisfied what I was being told was true.

But I think the real turning point in a non-personal assessment of the true climate that reigned in post-war America, one which looks squarely at the realities of life – especially those beneath the glossy surface of daily distractions of consumer life that continued at least until the Reagan era – has to have been the 1975 report of the Church Committee – officially the United States Senate

Select Committee to Study Governmental Operations with Respect to Intelligence Activities.

The report – which some say was softened because of Church's own presidential ambitions – was damning in the extreme, both with regard to specifics, such as the plans to assassinate foreign leaders, and to macro concerns that intelligence agencies – especially the CIA – had become free-wheeling agents of foreign policy, implicitly declaring their right, even their duty, to act as they saw fit in the conduct of covert operations. Put simply, these agencies had decided that they had the right and the duty to make political decisions and carry out even unethical, unlawful and immoral activities without recourse to review by the formal processes of American democracy.

Church himself expressed concern that such things as domestic surveillance might be used by agencies with legal competence only in foreign settings, but he did not go so far as to point out the obvious: *such agencies might, in the right circumstances, see it as their prerogative to bring all their methods to bear on the **domestic** setting if they themselves deemed the situation dire enough.*

I do not believe that the intelligence agencies as a whole, or even the CIA as a whole, made such a finding during the run-up to Dallas. There are those who do, and I can only say that history might eventually prove them right and me wrong. But if we are to understand the only American presidential assassination to take place since World War II, I think we have to recognize that it was entirely possible in the early 1960s, in the atmosphere of post-war triumphalism and at least an apparent threat to the all-important "American way of life", that a collection of the most radical of those who saw it as their right and their duty to protect that way of life by illegal and immoral means might have decided among themselves that the situation was, indeed, dire enough for them to turn their attention *and their methods* to the domestic setting.

Whether or not that perhaps relatively small fraction of the power elite was backed by the vast majority of that same elite or not is something that is beyond the scope of this discussion. The leap into grand conspiracy theories which involve the entirety of American history in the twentieth century so inflames the discussion, and requires such vast resources to investigate, I feel it needs to be dealt with further along the path we have set out on. I don't deny the

Ludlum-like possibilities, but I don't think they necessarily have an immediate bearing on determining what happened in Dallas. It seems likely that Allen Dulles acted in some oversight capacity for the operation; members of the military – very possibly Curtis LeMay – must have as well; there is strong evidence of the involvement of the Secret Service and the FBI, particularly in the cover-up (though in that respect we have to be careful to identify differing reasons for participating); the Mafia and the anti-Castro groups may have provided foot soldiers and certainly provided cheerleaders and moral support. And, since this all had to be bank-rolled with what must have been substantial sums of cash, the notions that Texas oil money was involved cannot be dismissed.[15]

However, the complicity and or culpability of those in the upper echelons of government, if it exists, will be far more difficult to uncover than that of those at the lower levels. So it is the aim of this discussion to assemble a picture of what happened at the level of the participants in the actual assassination of the president and those who can be plausibly identified as having acted as organizers and

---

[15] The question of whether there was any involvement on the part of Lyndon Johnson will be discussed further on.

"facilitators." However, there can be no question but that there were significant elements, some with substantial power, who could easily have assembled the means to a professional murder, even of an American president, and that their worldview was such that they could just as easily have justified their actions to themselves – *rationalized* is, perhaps, the better word – on the basis of "defense of America." Malcolm X famously said that JFK's shooting demonstrated that America's chickens had come home to roost. At the time he was derided and criticized for that remark; sadly, he was right on target.

Oswald

In the late Sixties, while the Vietnam War began to get into full swing, my cousin, perhaps four years older than me and a seaman in the US Navy, allegedly got into a fight in a bar on shore leave and, when the Shore Patrol were called, he punched one of them in the melee, fleeing the bar when he realized what he'd done. He was AWOL for six months, making no contact with friends or family, and then, unexpectedly and without any request on their part, my aunt and uncle received certification that he had been honorably discharged from the Navy. Over the course of the next three or four years, there were two reports of him having been sighted in carnivals that toured the country, my aunt and uncle received one strange phone call from a man using a transparently false Spanish accent who made references to my cousin, and then there was silence. Nothing was ever heard of or from him again.

My uncle, himself a Navy veteran from World War II, became convinced that his son had been recruited by Naval intelligence. I remember my uncle saying, in his best "don't give me that blarney" tone of voice, "You don't cold-cock the Shore Patrol, go AWOL and then get an honorable discharge that you haven't asked for." The odds are that my uncle was right.

The Office of Naval Intelligence, the ONI, was established in 1882 and, like other American military intelligence agencies, works hand in hand with its non-military counterparts. Moreover, ONI and its sister agencies provide recruitment opportunities for the "mother ship" of the US intelligence network, the CIA. Enlistees in the military may demonstrate what their superiors feel are exceptional aptitudes for intelligence work and, having been trained and used them during their tours of duty, they may be recommended for assignments after their "hitch" in the military has ended. On occasion, they might even be mustered out of the service under some pretext so as to allow them to assume responsibilities in the civilian intelligence community. My uncle remained convinced until his death that this had been the case with my cousin. It was most certainly true of a young Marine who, by his own admission, had been fascinated by the true-life story of a domestic, anti-communist spy hero who was the subject of a popular 1950s American book and television series, *I Led Three Lives*. The real-life spy in that series was named Herbert Philbrick.[16] The young Marine who had idolized

him was named Lee Oswald.

Oswald joined the Marines in 1956, when he was seventeen.

He had lived a difficult life up until then, residing in over twenty

locations around the country and attending a dozen schools; he also

suffered from dyslexia. But his high degree of native intelligence

was recognized as soon as he enlisted and he became a radar

operator, cleared by a security investigation to handle materials up to

and including "CONFIDENTIAL." (Confidential material is defined

by Army regulations as material which would cause damage or be

prejudicial to national security if made publicly available.) As

importantly, Oswald was assigned to the air base in Atsugi, Japan,

home to both U-2 surveillance activities over the Soviet Union and

"an innocuous group of buildings housing what was known only as

the 'Joint Technical Advisory Group'," in reality "the CIA main

operational base in the Far East."[17]

---

[16] Episodes from *I Led Three Lives* can be found on You Tube; Gene Rodenberry, later the creator of *Star Trek*, was one of the writers that gave the program its vibrancy. I too was a fan.

[17] Jim Marrs, *Crossfire* (New York: Basic Books, 2013); pp. 101-02. Much of what is recounted here is from Marrs' very helpful account of Oswald's life before the New Orleans-Dallas years.

During his stay at Atsugi, a number of incidents took place reminiscent of my cousin's apparent moment of deviance – including a bar brawl – which, as has been pointed out by others, allowed him to be absent from normal duties for what appeared to be time in the brig. But in parallel with the absences, Oswald developed a remarkable proficiency in Russian – no small achievement for a high school dropout – and it has been suggested that he followed a military language course, perhaps even at what is now called the Defense Language Institute in Monterey.[18] Among Oswald's various activities while at Atsugi seems to have been the frequenting of an expensive geisha bar in Tokyo at the request of his

---

[18] Full disclosure: This author served on the faculty of the Monterey Institute of International Studies from 1978 until 1989 – during which time John McCone became a member of the Board of Trustees. MIIS, DLI and the Naval Postgraduate School were often mistaken for one another, or assumed to be one entity, but MIIS (now the Middlebury Institute of International Studies) has always been a private institution; my colleagues and I used to joke about rumors we were funded by the CIA, given that we all accepted sub-par salaries in order to work in a very satisfying educational environment. The author occasionally gave invited lectures to students of Polish, Czech and Serbo-Croatian at DLI because of his experiences in those areas as a Fulbright professor and a USIS lecturer; at no time did I interact with the American intelligence community during those years, nor was I ever approached about collecting intelligence in those countries – a request I would have dismissed out of hand. It's also worth noting that at least one author – Anthony Summers – has claimed that the DLI provided "highly sophisticated crash courses." In fact, the high-level courses have always been provided by the Foreign Service Institute in Washington D.C. DLI's courses have always been rather "assembly line" instruction for low-level military personnel, many enlisted men and women.

superiors, where it was feared U-2 pilots and others might be allowing themselves to be plied for classified information. Oswald's medical record includes the odd mention of him having contracted gonorrhea – normally considered as misconduct subject to disciplinary measures – with the notation, "Origin: In the line of duty, not due to misconduct."

Along with Oswald's sudden interest in and proficiency with Russian, there developed what seemed to some an unconvincing sympathy with Marxism and communism. One of his roommates, James Botelho, later appointed a Justice Court judge in 1968 in the State of California, has said that he felt that Oswald was, in fact, deeply opposed to Soviet communism and that the pro-Soviet remarks he began making after he served a month and a half brig sentence (during which only one person could remember seeing him at the brig – once, and in civilian clothes) were part of a persona that Oswald was developing for an eventual intelligence assignment. One of Oswald's colleagues at Atsugi, David Bucknell, has said that in 1959, about six months before Oswald's September 11 discharge, he, Oswald and several marines – then at the El Toro base in California – were interviewed by the military Criminal Investigation

Division and recruited for an anti-communist intelligence operation against Cuba. Oswald was selected for a number of interviews and he told Bucknell that he had been chosen to go to Russia on an intelligence mission and would be discharged from the Marines.

Inexplicably, Bucknell was never interviewed by the Warren Commission, though Botelho was. But in late August of 1959, Oswald applied for a hardship discharge on the improbable basis of an injury his mother had sustained when a box of candy had fallen on her nose the previous December; two weeks later – and to all his comrades' surprise (perhaps, one suspects, excepting Bucknell) – it was approved. One week before the approval, Oswald had applied for a passport, stating in the application that he intended to travel to Cuba and the Soviet Union, and he was issued the passport the day before his discharge papers arrived. Then, after the briefest of stays with his mother, Oswald booked passage aboard a freighter sailing out of New Orleans for Le Havre, and embarked on the voyage on September 20.

Discontinuities in stamps in his passport and reservations at hotels in London, where he went after disembarking at Southampton, and Helsinki make it appear that Oswald may have used military transport, since no commercial flights seem to tally with the date when he made the then-one day trip, but he arrived in Finland on October 10, was granted a visa to the Soviet Union in the record time of two days (at least a week was normal) and arrived in Moscow on October 16. Thus began Lee Oswald's nearly three years as an apparent American defector to the Soviet Union – a stay that would contribute largely, and in numerous and contradictory ways, to theories about his involvement or non-involvement in the murder of John Kennedy.

Given the images that often come to mind, both when we talk about intelligence agents and defectors – especially Cold War defectors – it's worth stopping for a moment to examine what defection, or defection as a guise for intelligence operations, might mean.

We're all wise enough in the ways of the world – as was not the case in the 1950s and 60s – to know that the smooth, cool handsome James Bond prototype for the modern spy, an image that beguiled even JFK himself, is a fiction. Moreover, the "other side's" wily, cunning, ruthless counterpart to the Bond character is much the same: a portrait designed to involve and entertain us. In many respects, those involved in intelligence operations are – and often see themselves – as career professionals plying the waters of their craft in sometimes all too human fashion, and without the verve and panache books and films give to them.[19]

However, knowing what we have come to know about the intelligence community since the revelations of the Church committee, we can say that many of the upper level intelligence personnel saw themselves as "above the law" – to use the infamous phrase of Fawn Hall, the assistant to Oliver North during the Iran-Contra affair – and we might well think that the foot soldier-agents in these organizations would be the same: self-justifying practitioners who imagine they can use immoral means to moral ends. No doubt, this characterization would fit many in their profession. But there is yet another profile one might propose.

---

[19] My sole contact with the CIA came when I was interviewed many years ago about a former student who was applying for entry into the foreign service and thus had to undergo a security check. I was astounded at how dull and unresponsive to any of my attempts to be congenial the agent was. To characterize him as a tepid, plodding bureaucrat would be to put it mildly. (Interestingly, I was struck the same way by my first encounter with a Communist functionary when I arrived in Czechoslovakia as a Fulbright professor and had to introduce myself to a Ministry of Education official. The similarity between the two gave me much to think about over the coming years.)

During the early days of the student movements of the 1960s, I well recall a certain type of young, male activist that stood out against the backdrop of the multitude of those of us who were more inclined towards, as we said in those times, the world of "sex, drugs and rock 'n roll." These relatively few, distinctly different characters were often a bit older – in their late twenties, when most of us were in our early twenties – were generally clean-cut, more mature, and had spent some years doing something else before entering the university, if only having completed military service. But some had been in the Peace Corps, in VISTA – or had even participated in volunteer social work, like voter registration in the South. They were often quietly – sometimes almost naively – idealistic in their dedication, not only to the goals of social justice and government transparency that were being espoused in demonstrations and teach-ins, but to larger goals that sometimes had religious (Quaker, perhaps) or mystical (Buddhist in some cases) origins and which bespoke of a very sincere commitment to the well-being of all humankind.[20]

---

[20] I remember speaking with one such young man who was in the National Guard during the face-off between the Justice Department and Governor George Wallace over the integration of the University of Alabama. After a particularly contentious

As I did my work on the "second" Oswald in 1967 – the notion that there were impersonators pretending to be Oswald at various times and for not entirely clear reasons – I found myself being reminded of these young men and their idealism. And years later, when the internet made it possible to go back and review the footage of Lee Oswald from the 1962-63 period, that comparison came back with considerable force. In particular, the facial expressions we see when Oswald encounters reporters during the midnight "press conference" at 12:10 on the morning of November 23 revealed something I felt was very akin to the earnest, slightly older idealists I'd remembered from the Sixties. Oswald is asked if he killed the President, and he responds "No, I've not been charged with that. In fact, nobody has said that to me yet." As he continues one of the reporters tells him he has, indeed, been so charged. The noise in the room requires the reporter's remark to be repeated, and when Oswald absorbs it, a look of disgust comes across his face, but the look is mixed with great emotional fatigue *and* a kind of

---

teach-in during which it was agreed that a follow-up demonstration would be postponed until college officials could respond to demands that were being made, he expressed his satisfaction with the outcome, saying quietly, "We have to learn to talk to one another before we start shouting."

endurance that is still firmly in place, but waning as the burden he carries becomes heavier and heavier.

While there's no proof that what I've described is what Oswald felt, I've offered the description to the one living person who knew him intimately, Judyth Vary Baker – about whose account we will have much more to say further on – and she thinks it accurate. Moreover, it gives us a deeper insight into how Lee Oswald thought about himself and his role in the intelligence activities he had undertaken.

Baker tells us of an Oswald who detested racism, but detested Castro, an Oswald who was, indeed, Marxist in many of his leanings but unwavering in his opposition to Soviet communism – and, tellingly, a man who admired JFK. And, most especially, she describes a young man who was extremely idealistic and dedicated to doing what he could to further the goals of peace and social justice that he had come, through extensive reading, to believe in. *This*, it seems to me, is the Lee Oswald that we need to keep in mind as we try to understand his role in the events that would lead to Dealey Plaza: an idealistic, intelligent and thoughtful autodidact who, in the Cold War climate which dominated the world as he

reached maturity, chose action in support of his beliefs, in effect –
and oh, so ironically – asking what he could do for his country, not
what it could do for him.

Moreover, the determination to follow the code of silence
which has always been implicit in the intelligence community,
explains both the look of grim determination and emotional
exhaustion we see on Oswald's face at learning he's been charged
with the assassination; but it also explains a great deal of both what
he does and what he seems to do in the years between his Marine
enlistment and his death. For, while intelligence operatives are not
likely to be either suave or cavalier in the style of Ian Fleming's
hero, they most certainly must be adept at disguise and obfuscation –
to the point where they may regularly and reflexively leave false
clues in even the smallest matters, knowing intuitively when such
maneuvers might help obscure their real actions and intentions.
Oswald's apparent oscillation between the role of Soviet
sympathizer and the anti-Castro and pro-Castro positions he took in
his New Orleans and Dallas activities becomes quite understandable
in the light of what he and Baker would refer to as his "Scarlet
Pimpernel" role.

Thus it can be difficult, at least at our current level of knowledge, to understand exactly what Lee Oswald was up to in the period after he became involved in intelligence. We are, for instance, unable to say with any certainty what his "mission" in going to the Soviet Union may have been. At one end of the spectrum, he may have been expected to ferret out information at, for instance, the Foreign Language Institute in Minsk, or the Soviet espionage school that also existed there. At the other end, it's entirely possible that his mission failed or was called off; this might account for the "changed man" – cold and unfriendly – Marina said he became when they returned to the US. We just don't know.[21]

Nor do we have a very clear picture of what Oswald's real activities were between the time he, Marina and their newborn daughter returned – arriving in New Jersey on June 13, 1962, 18 months before the assassination – and the initiation of his activities in Dallas and New Orleans. On several occasions, though the facts are unclear and were mostly ignored by the Warren Commission,

---

[21] There is growing evidence that the CIA feared the Soviets had learned about their top secret U-2 spy plane through a "mole" in the CIA itself. Oswald may have been a "dangle": he offered his knowledge about the plane to see if the Soviet's took the bait. If they did not, it might confirm that they had a mole and did not need more information.

Oswald had contact with the FBI and perhaps the CIA soon after his return – passed off, when they were brought to light, as routine debriefings of an American who had lived in the USSR.

He and Marina first settled in Ft. Worth, where Lee's mother resided, and they began to circulate with Russian expatriates in the area, especially George de Mohrenschildt, a White Russian oil geologist with a colorful past who sometimes moved in intelligence circles. De Mohrenschildt and his wife took the Oswalds under their wing, George and Lee seemed to get along quite famously despite the contrast between George's sophisticated background and Lee's plebian upbringing, and when the de Mohrenschildts became aware of tensions, and even apparent violence, between Lee and Marina, George is said to have urged Lee to quit his job as a sheet metal worker and look for work in nearby Dallas. Lee did so; and very quickly, and apparently with de Mohrenschildt's help, Oswald was employed by a photographic firm in Dallas, Jaggars-Chiles-Stovall, which, among other things, did work for the military – including developing composite photos taken by U-2 pilots.[22] Oswald seems

---

[22] Though there appears to be no direct evidence to support a connection between Oswald, the firm and the event, early October was when JFK was first shown U-2 photos that indicated missile positions were being established in Cuba.

to have been very motivated in the job and, in the process, acquired photographic equipment that would have been far beyond the reach of someone at his pay scale. It could well be that, at the time, he was being given a kind of "basic training" for a new assignment. Marina joined him in early November, though their relationship remained strained.

For the six months during which Oswald worked at the photographic firm, nothing out of the ordinary seems to have taken place, with one possible exception. According to Marina, Lee returned home one evening in an agitated state and told her he had taken a shot at General Edwin Walker, a well-known extreme-right wing activist, but that he thought had failed to kill him. It has been suggested, but not proven, that Oswald was acting at the behest of Mac Wallace, an alleged hit-man who worked for LBJ, in a test of Lee's marksmanship.[23] But no one other than Marina has ever alleged Oswald had anything to do with the shooting.

---

[23] See Barr McClellan, *Blood, Money and Power: How LBJ Killed JFK* (New York: Skyhorse Publishing, 2011), p. 22. Intriguingly, Wallace's palm print is said to have been the only identifiable print found in the so-called "sniper's nest" in the Texas School Book Depository that didn't correspond to that of a TSBD employee or a police officer.

The Walker incident took place a day after Oswald had finally left Jaggars-Chiles-Stovall, and from that time until his departure for New Orleans, Oswald collected unemployment insurance on which he and his family lived. The de Morhenschildts left Dallas for Haiti in June and never had contact with Oswald again. It seems plausible that Geroge de Mohrenschildt had been working, perhaps not as a "handler" – that is, someone who is giving direct orders to a CIA operative – but as a "cut-out" – someone who acts as intermediary between the agency and an operative.[24] If so, one would expect to see some kind of change accompanying the de Mohrenschildts departure and, indeed, changes begin in April that seem to suggest that wheels have begun turning that would power the killing machine's inevitable progress to Dealey Plaza.

---

[24] No evidence has ever been presented that Oswald was a *bone fide* employee of the CIA. He seems to have been, as many were, a contract agent or "asset" who worked for the Agency under the table and under the radar; he operated strictly on a need-to-know basis – meaning his knowledge of what he was involved in was highly compartmentalized – and he was paid on a cash basis. See John Newman's *Oswald and the CIA* (Baltimore: Skyhorse, 2008)

IV

New Orleans

In what would have been the waning days of George de Mohrenschidt's role as a "cut-out" for Lee Oswald – if, indeed, he was one – there was a clear change in Oswald's activities that would suggest a new kind of oversight had been put into place, most probably a "handler": someone who worked directly with the agency and who issued marching orders to the asset. We'll come back to the question of this person's identity in the next section, but it is clear that the de Mohrenschidts' departure signaled a change to a more active and purposeful mode than had been the case up until then.

Towards the end of his first stay in Dallas, Oswald began to write letters to the Fair Play for Cuba Committee's headquarters in New York. The Committee had been set up in 1960 to provide support for the Cuban Revolution, and counted among its members such notables as Jean Paul Sartre, Allen Ginsberg and James

Baldwin. Oswald wrote to the chair of the committee, V.T. Lee, praising the committee and Castro, asking for membership forms and leaflets and advice on "tactics." V.T. Lee's response, cautioning against stirring unnecessary opposition with strong measures, could almost be seen as a guide book in reverse for the often provocative activities Oswald would soon undertake. Oswald also announced to Marina that they were moving to New Orleans, where he had family and claimed he would have better prospects of finding employment, and they were literally packed and ready to start their trip when Ruth Paine, a woman who had befriended them as a member of the Russian circles, convinced Lee to let Marina and their daughter stay with her; she, too, was living apart from her husband.[25]

So, Lee set out alone for New Orleans. There, he became involved in more Fair Play for Cuba activities that appear to have been staged to give him the appearance of a disgruntled, and rather eccentric, American supporter of Castro. Most researchers agree that this was a process of "sheep-dipping": taking an operative and

---

[25] There are doubts about the Paines' real motives for befriending the Oswalds. Ruth Paine's sister worked for the CIA and it has been suggested that Paine herself acted as an occasional informant. Much of the material incriminating Oswald after the assassination was found in her garage. (See Cox, *The President and the Provocateur* (Harpenden, Herts: Oldcastle, 2013; pp. 129-31.)

giving him (and sometimes her) the appearance of something they were not – in this case, a supporter of Fidel Castro. Given that the addresses on the flyers he handed out were the same building as the offices of Guy Banister, a former FBI agent and now deeply involved in anti-Castro activities, and that Oswald was frequently seen in those offices, it's clear that there was an attempt to portray Oswald as pro-Castro, and that he participated fully in that charade.

But why? For years, there was no clear answer to this question, though the apparent disparity between his FPCC activities – including leafleting a US aircraft carrier docked in New Orleans and engaging in other leafleting that ended in a physical confrontation with anti-Castro Cubans, leading to everyone's arrest – caused some to believe he was, indeed, a "lone nut," others to believe that he was trying to discredit the FPCC, and still others to assert that Oswald's (second) charade as a communist sympathizer was part of an intricate CIA plot, the aim of which remained obscure. It was not until three decades after the assassination that the fog obscuring these episodes began to lift, and the dimensions of what was taking place in New Orleans, and in Dallas, began to come into focus.

In her game-changing *Me and Lee*,[26] Judyth Vary Baker recounts how, as a teen prodigy in cancer research, she had been recruited by one of the country's foremost cancer specialists, Alton Ochsner – former president of the American Cancer Society and founder of the Ochsner Clinic in New Orleans – nominally to help with the clinic's efforts to find a cure for cancer, for which Baker had demonstrated a rare gift in her high school and undergraduate university work. However, when she came to New Orleans, a nineteen-year old, in May of 1963 – only weeks after Oswald had arrived from Dallas – for what was to be a summer as a research assistant in Ochsner's clinic followed by guaranteed enrollment in the medical school of Tulane, where Ochsner had great influence, she found something frighteningly different.

Over the course of several days, during which she first met Lee Oswald in what appeared to be a chance encounter at the Post Office, but which she now believes to have been a reconnoitering task he was given, Baker learned from Oswald, David Ferrie – a pilot, CIA operative and amateur researcher, among many other things – and eventually from Dr. Mary Sherman, another famous

---

[26] Walterville: Trine Day, 2011.

cancer specialist who worked with Ochsner, that they were working on developing a strain of "galloping" mutant cancer that would kill a subject within days and that this bioweapon would be used to kill Fidel Castro. Because she had grown up in Florida and had known Cubans from refugee families who were virulently opposed to the Castro regime, Baker accepted the notion that Castro himself was a menace to freedom and democracy and had to be dealt with. But as someone who had committed herself to curing cancer – most especially because it had taken her grandmother, a beloved mentor and others she knew – she felt deeply ambivalent about participating in what was, essentially, a murder plot, no matter how justifiable its goal might make it appear.

In a luncheon with Ferrie and Dr. Sherman at Sherman's apartment, when the entire scenario had been laid out for her and she showed her hesitation, Ferrie dropped a bomb that pushed Baker to the edge of believing she'd entered some dark parallel universe – which, indeed, she had. In essence, and speaking cryptically, Ferrie made it clear that the anti-Castro Cuban community, especially the militants who had trained to retake the island, many having lost friends and family at the Bay of Pigs or in the revolution itself, were enraged over JFK's failure to bring Castro to heel, both in the Bay of Pigs affair and later in the Missile Crisis, and that they were plotting the President's assassination. Ferrie said explicitly that it was his hope, as well as Dr. Sherman's and Lee Oswald's, that the death of Castro would assuage the more radical Cubans and cool things off enough to save Kennedy's life.

Only nineteen, Baker's head swam at the thought of what she had stumbled into, and though she was assured she could walk away and suffer no consequences of a refusal to participate, she vacillated. And by this time she and Oswald had begun to feel a strong attraction toward one another. Lost in a large city where she knew no one, she clung to him and what seemed his very gentlemanly and sincere behavior with her. Moreover, she learned that he was deeply involved in The Project, as it was called. He would be the one who would take the cancer cells, once they had been developed, to Mexico City to be turned over to a sympathetic Cuban opposed to the regime who would then deliver the "product" into the hands of those in Cuba who would put the assassination plan into action. In a worst case scenario, Oswald would carry the product into Cuba himself – and thus his sheep-dipping pro-Castro activities.

Filled with conflicting emotions, Baker says that the scientist in her was awakened when she was shown the cancer cells that had been developed and the unheard of rates of growth they demonstrated and she became involved in The Project almost reflexively. She and Oswald took cover jobs at the O'Reilly Coffee Company, arranged through Ochsner, which would allow them to spend a good deal of time working at Ferrie's apartment, as well as at Sherman's, breeding mice, injecting them with cancer cells, "harvesting" the tumors produced, subjecting them to radiation and injecting the new strains into subsequent generations of mice.

As the days progressed, Judyth and Lee became more and more involved with one another – even though Judyth's fiancée had arrived and they had gone through a short wedding ceremony before he left for work on an oil rig in the Gulf, and Marina had arrived with their daughter to stay with Lee. The intimacy that grew between Judyth and Lee led him to make more and more revelations to her about his work in covert operations and about his connections with the New Orleans-based Mafia – connections that went back to his uncle, who worked for Carlos Marcello, the head of the Mafia in New Orleans. Lee professed dislike for that side of his activities, as he did for working with Guy Banister to uncover communist sympathizers on local college campuses; but he said that he had to maintain various unsavory connections that would prove valuable in his larger mission, which he never fully revealed to Judyth.

Perhaps the most striking revelation to come from Baker's account of that summer, at least to those who know the often fragmentary evidence of Oswald's time in New Orleans, was the explanation she provides for what was known as "the Clinton episode."

A number of witnesses claim to have seen Oswald in the company of two men, all of them in a black Cadillac, in Clinton, Louisiana in late August of that year. It had been reported that Oswald made an attempt to register to vote, allegedly because, he told the registrar, he would have a better chance of obtaining work at the nearby Jackson State Hospital. The episode took place in the midst of a voter drive by the Congress of Racial Equality that summer, and puzzled researchers have wondered – particularly after Jim Garrison's investigation alleged that the driver of the car was Clay Shaw – whether this might have been some aspect of the FBI's COINTELPRO attempts to infiltrate civil rights groups.

In fact, Baker says, by late August "the Product" had reached sufficient virulence to be ready for testing on a human subject. She had been told that volunteers at the state penitentiary with terminal diseases had agreed to be subjects in the test, and Oswald, Ferrie and Shaw – a respected New Orleans businessman covertly involved in CIA and anti-Castro activities, later charged in the Garrison investigation – were waiting to join the motorcade with the prisoner. Baker had trained Ferrie and Oswald in how to handle the "product" and Ferrie would give the prisoner the injection once he had arrived. As Oswald recounted the story to Baker, during the long wait for the motorcade, watching blacks being rejected for spurious reasons by the voting registrar, he made a bet with Ferrie and Shaw that he could get better treatment than the blacks if he stood in line. He won the bet.

But a far more critical moment for Baker – indeed, a turning point – came when she learned, first from David Ferrie, later from inspecting the prisoner's charts herself, that the prisoner did not have a terminal disease, did not know he was being injected with deadly, "galloping" cancer cells designed as a bioweapon, and that he had been chosen primarily because he was Cuban and about the same height and weight as Fidel Castro. Feeling she had been duped into participating in a project that had much darker aspects than she'd been told (she also came to believe that not one, but several prisoners had been injected), she wrote a note of protest to Dr. Ochsner over the unethical and illegal practices she'd discovered.

Baker's note – and specifically the fact that she had put something in writing: a taboo in The Project – made her *persona non grata* in Ochsner's eyes; he responded with fury. She was told to wrap up her final duties and that the guarantees of entry into Tulane's medical school he'd made were off the table. David Ferrie warned her that her fall from grace in Ochsner's eyes, especially given everything she had learned in her three-plus months with The Project, meant that she was a marked woman and had to disappear. She returned to Florida, where she kept in touch with Oswald, with whom she now had plans to escape to South America at the first opportunity, and Ferrie, who had become a friend and protector, via an elaborate phone system which used Mafia gambling telephone lines.

In the meantime, Oswald made his famous trip to Mexico City – another episode for which explanations remained elusive to researchers – to hand off the "product," which had now undergone

the tests successfully, for use on Castro. However Baker, whose

knowledge of the activities in New Orleans during this time came in

fits and starts from her telephone conversations with Oswald and

Ferrie, now wonders whether or not the Mexico trip – unknown to

Oswald – also had the covert aim of setting him up to take the fall

for the assassination, something he had already begun to suspect

might be afoot. His contact in Mexico City never arrived, his

attempts to get a visa to take "the Product" to Cuba himself came to

nothing, and suggestions to him that, after the delivery of "the

Product" he would stay on in Mexico on a new assignment (which

would also allow him to rendezvous with Baker), were reneged upon

for reasons that seemed improbable. But his trip to the Cuban

consulate, and subsequent misleading information provided about his

Mexico trip, would allow conspirators in the assassination to use him

to make a connection between JFK's murder and the Cuban regime,

if that seemed a plausible story to put out.[27] He returned to Dallas,

---

[27] Though that story was allowed to circulate only as an exercise in misdirection, it was – ironically – what LBJ and perhaps many others used to justify making Oswald the center of the "sole assassin/lone nut" explanation that the Warren Commission would espouse. To do otherwise, Johnson argued in persuading Earl Warren to head the commission, would risk revealing Cuban involvement – which

deeply depressed and increasingly convinced that he would be made a patsy for the assassination. His handler told him simply that a Mexico assignment might come later, but that for now he was to infiltrate and keep an eye on the activities of "a bunch of right-wing nuts interested in killing Kennedy."[28]

Lee Oswald returned from Mexico on October 3, and two mornings later the *Dallas Morning News* announced JFK's plan to visit the city. The curtain was about to go up on final act of this revenger's tragedy, planned by an elite, executed by foot soldiers and signifying – perhaps – the most important turning point in the history of American democracy in the 20th century . . . and beyond.

---

could start the dominoes falling towards American invasion of the island and nuclear war with the Soviet Union.

[28] Baker, p. 505.

V

The Road to Dallas

The events which followed Lee Oswald's return from Mexico need to be contextualized within the frame of the larger conspiracy which brought everything to a head in Dealey Plaza. In order to do that, we need to establish, as best one can, what the make-up of the conspiracy was. That's no easy task. The overwhelming bulk of the evidence collected over five decades strongly suggests the involvement, as we have said, of elements of the CIA. That last phrase is important: there is evidence of individuals being involved, but there is no evidence that the entire agency was – and, in the end, the very notion that it was would be preposterous, given the "need to know" basis upon which agents worked and the unlikelihood that anyone outside the magic circle of conspirators would be informed of what was going to take place.

The best place to begin a reconstruction of the structure of the conspiracy would be a point at which we might find an intersection between the various groups who had an interest in seeing the President killed. Such an intersection exists in the person of David Attlee Phillips.

It has long been suspected by researchers that Phillips, an CIA agent for twenty-five years who ended his career as chief of operations in the Western Hemisphere – nominally meaning South and Central America and the Caribbean, given that the CIA was technically forbidden to conduct domestic operations – was somehow involved in conspiracy to kill Kennedy. Phillips was involved in the US coup that overthrew the democratically-elected government in Guatemala in 1954 and was said to have been involved in the assassination of Chilean exile Orlando Letelier in Washington D.C. in 1973. More importantly, it was long suspected that Phillips was involved in the CIA's JM/WAVE activities in support of anti-Castro Cubans in Florida, and specifically in the Alpha 66 group that was tasked with the assassination of Castro.

Gaeton Fonzi, a journalist and an investigator for both the Church committee and the HSCA, focused specifically on the links between the CIA and anti-Castro groups and in 1976 struck up an especially fruitful relationship with Antonio Veciana, a former Havana banker and one of the founders of Alpha 66, who for thirteen years worked for the CIA in its attempts to assassinate Castro, his "handler" being a man who called himself "Maurice Bishop." From his work with the committee, Fonzi felt certain that "Bishop" was actually David Phillips, but he could never get Veciana to confirm the fact, even after arranging an encounter between the two of them in which Phillips was so visibly nervous his hands could be seen shaking throughout.

Fonzi's failure to get confirmation that Phillips was "Bishop" particularly frustrated him because Venciana claimed that he had seen Lee Oswald in the company of "Bishop" in Dallas in September or October of 1963, when Venciana happened to arrive a few minutes early for a meeting that had been scheduled with "Bishop" at the Southland Center. Venciana only spent a few brief minutes with the two men before the man he claimed was Oswald was sent off by "Bishop," but when Venciana saw the pictures of Oswald immediately after the assassination, he had no doubts that it was the same man and remained absolutely certain of Oswald's identity when Fonzi interviewed him several times during Fonzi's tenure as an HSAC investigator in the mid-70s.

During the very tense encounter Fonzi set up between Phillips and Venciana, the latter had glared intently at the former throughout, but Venciana would not confirm that Phillips was "Bishop." When asked the question, Venciana would only respond, with a steely edge, "No . . . but he knows."[29] And it wasn't until 40 years later, in 2014, that Venciana acknowledged to a gathering of researchers at the Assassination Archives and Research Center that Phillips was, indeed, "Bishop" and that Venciana had hidden this fact out of a misguided sense of honor and fear for the safety of his family.[30] He elaborated on his belief that, when one put together all of the small pieces of the puzzle he was exposed to – conversations, oblique references, and repeated references by Bishop/Phillips to the problem that JFK represented to the safety of the United States –

---

[29] Gaeton Fonzi, *The Last Investigation* (New York: Skyhorse, 2013); p. 169.
[30] The entire presentation, including Venciana's definitive confirmation that "Bishop" and Phillips were one and the same man, can be viewed on You Tube: https://www.youtube.com/watch?v=gY-psk_aPhU Sadly, Fonzi did not live to see his strong suspicion that Bishop was Phillips confirmed.

Phillips was near the center, if not himself the center, of a successful plot to kill Kennedy and that elements of the CIA, the Mafia, the anti-Castro Cubans and the US military were involved.

Veciana's remarks have powerful consequences for any attempt to shape an understanding of what took place in Dealey Plaza – not least because, as one questioner at the conference comments, even intelligence reports on Veciana that have since been made public describe him as "straight, honest and truthful." But let's stay for the time being with the revelation that confirmed what had been Gaeton Fonzi's conviction up until his death of complications from Parkinson's disease in 2012: David Attlee Phillips, at the time of the assassination the CIA's Chief of Cuban Operations, met with Lee Oswald in Dallas in the run-up to the assassination. Moreover, Judyth Baker recalls hearing from David Ferrie that Lee had made a trip to Dallas at the time Venciana describes his encounter with Oswald. She also says that Oswald mentioned his handler on several occasions, referring to him – as the handler had himself, at first – as "Mr. B.", then "Benton" or "Benson." And in describing their final phone conversation, on November 20, Baker says:

"Know how we wondered who my handler was?" Lee whispered. "Mr. B? Benson, Benton, or Bishop? Well, he's from Fort Worth, so it has to be Phillips . . . Phillips is behind this. I need you to remember that name . . . David Atlee Phillips."[31]

The implications are quite clear: Phillips/Bishop had been working with anti-Castro Cubans for some time, he was now the CIA's chief of operations for that country, he was seen in the company of Oswald just after Oswald's return from Mexico, and Oswald himself identified him as his handler. Phillips is, thus, the lynchpin that links the assassination with the CIA; exactly how we'll look at in a moment. But it is worth speculating about who else might have been involved, for it is unlikely that even a chief of operations would be able to mount the assassination of a sitting president, and Veciana himself insists that there was a "decision" made by "a group of people" to kill Kennedy, implying that Phillips was the point man in the operation.

We can only speculate, but it is not hard to come up with highly plausible candidates. Allen Dulles must be placed high in the

---

[31] Baker, *op.cit.*

list of any suspects. As has been said, he had helped shape the CIA from its earliest days, was appointed its first civilian director in 1952 and had been its equivalent of J. Edgar Hoover at the FBI ever since. But the fiasco of the Bay of Pigs, for which the CIA had rightly been seen as a perpetrator that had vastly overreached itself, led JFK both to mistrust and detest the CIA, to foresee its dismemberment and to fire Dulles. Had the CIA been just another branch of the American civil service, that would have been an unremarkable act. But, particularly given what we now know, thanks to the Church committee and others, about the way in which American intelligence agencies operated in those days – particularly with regard to the gross impropriety in their covertly formulating and carrying out foreign policy – the decapitating of the snake the CIA had become did not guarantee that it had become incapacitated. On the contrary, given its self-justifying view of itself as the court of last resort in protecting "the American way of life," one is not hard-pressed to imagine the rage that would have coursed through the veins of the agency when Dulles was fired and the emergence of Kennedy and his brother as the targets of that rage. Dulles' assent to an attempt to remove JFK from office, albeit criminally and traitorously, would have been all it would have taken to start the wheels in motion. And, given Dulles own view of himself as central to the CIA's "mission," it would hardly be surprising if he himself took an active role in undermining the Agency's perceived enemy.

Military candidates for involvement in such an operation are not hard to come by: JFK's relations with the Joint Chief of Staff were notoriously bad, and none worse than with the Air Force Chief of Staff, Curtis Le May. Le May was a highly successful, rather pudgy and cigar-smoking commander in Europe and the Far East[32] during World War II, but was described by Robert McNamara – a subordinate during the war, and later Secretary of Defense – as "extraordinarily belligerent, many thought brutal." The two clashed often when McNamara became his titular boss.

But the clashes between Le May and JFK were, if anything, more intense, and sometimes smacked of insubordination. Le May pushed hard for use of nuclear weapons in Berlin and Southeast Asia, called The Cuban Missile Crisis the country's "greatest defeat" and baited the President repeatedly in meetings. On one occasion,

---

[32] Le May directed the firebombing of Japanese cities, using incendiary bombs and napalm, at the cost of a hundred thousand civilian lives.

Kennedy lost his customary *sang froid* and gave as good as he got; it took place during the Missile Crisis and the discussion of a blockade to pressure the Cubans and the Soviets without risk of war:

Le May: I think that a blockade and political talk would be considered by a lot of our friends an neutrals as bein' a pretty weak response to this . . . In other words, you're in a pretty bad fix at the present time."

Kennedy: What'd you say?

Le May: I say, you're in a pretty bad fix.

Kennedy: [laughing hollowly] Well, you're in there with me.[33]

Later, Kennedy would say to Kenny O'Donnell, "Can you imagine Le May saying a thing like that? These brass hats have one great advantage in their favor. If we listen to them, and do what they want us to do, none of us will be alive later to tell them they were wrong."[34]

Le May was mysteriously absent from Washington on the day of the assassination, but managed to return, apparently just in time to attend the autopsy of the President at Bethesda. One of the

---

[33] Quote taken from Dallek (p. 344) and Douglass (p. 22).
[34] Dallek (p. 345).

attending doctors told an assistant to ask a member of the gallery to put out the cigar he was smoking. The person's response was to blow smoke in the assistant's face; the assistant said he was certain the man was Le May.

There were others in and recently retired from the military who would have been happy to see JFK removed from office – among them, General Earl Cabell, brother of the mayor of Dallas and fired by JFK after the Bay of Pigs, and General Edwin Walker, a far-right winger who was fired by Kennedy for requiring his troops read right-wing literature, among them. And no doubt there were others, all of whom could provide moral support for a plot, and some of whom might even provide logistical support as well.[35]

But perhaps the most intriguing of the support groups was the Mafia, in part because of the way in which their shadows seem to flit in and out of the most plausible narratives, in part because of the links between them and some of the major players – Ruby, Ferrie

---

[35] Though there is no evidence that the military played a role in the Dealey Plaza shooting itself, it may have helped in a number of logistical ways – among them the reported order for the 112th Military Intelligence Group's supplemental Presidential protection team at Fort Sam Houston to stand down during Kennedy's Dallas visit, despite this being a violation of normal security preparations for a Presidential visit.

and even Oswald himself. In the case of Oswald, everything we know from Baker and from the record of Oswald's activities suggests that his contacts were, as he told her, primarily part of a debt he felt he owed to his uncle, who had acted as surrogate father for Lee from his youth,[36] and as a practical "tool of his trade." But at the higher levels of the Mob, the potential for animosity towards the Kennedys was explosive.

The Mafia suffered greatly from the loss of casinos and other rackets in Cuba after Castro took over. New Orleans, in particular, which had been the gateway for much of the money that flowed between the mainland and the island, was hurt. But even more importantly, the Kennedy brothers had, as we have said, targeted organized crime as one group of "bad guys" they would run out of town, and mere months after JFK took the oath of office, federal agents acting at the behest of the President's brother arrested Carlos Marcello – the "godfather" of organized crime in New Orleans – and

---

[36] Charles "Dutz" Murret was a low-level operative in Carlos' Marcello's crime syndicate. Lee once told Baker he had been deeply gratified by a subtle sign that Dutz had given him that expressed his understanding that Lee was involved in intelligence work on behalf of the country and that he approved.

unceremoniously put him on a plane for Guatemala without observing any of the niceties, or legalities, of official deportation.

Given the time-honored tradition of Mafia bosses in which countless lawyers would file countless briefs to postpone legal action against them seemingly forever, RFK's tactics may have made sense. But they violated a cardinal rule of the mob by publically humiliating a member of "the family." From that point on, all-but-open war had been declared, and – as Marcello's later remark, "We should have killed Bobby" revealed – there was a blood feud that demanded revenge.[37] What's more, the Justice Department was no less diligent in its prosecution of the war on organized crime in Miami, where the likes of boss Santos Trafficante, who had lost important assets to Castro's revolution and was deeply involved in plans to assassinate Castro, complained loudly and repeatedly about the Kennedys "persecution" and is alleged to have told an associate that JFK would never be reelected because he "was going to be hit." Robert Maheu – former FBI agent and later attorney for Howard Hughes – allegedly acted as a go-between for the CIA and

---

[37] Marcello had reportedly donated half a million dollars, via Jimmy Hoffa, to the campaign of Richard Nixon in 1960.

approached Johnny Roselli of the Chicago mob, with a $1.5 million offer for Castro's murder; Roselli declined to take payment, but attempts to kill Castro by the mob were undertaken and reportedly overseen by Roselli.

We'll take a look at the role that organized crime may have played in the actual operation to kill JFK further on. However, it's important at this point to reemphasize the fact that there was likely never a "meeting of the dons" in which the assassination was planned, or even given the go-ahead. There was more than enough sentiment – and animus – in organized crime to support the assassination of the President. Most likely, heads probably nodded their assent to communications from others in the Mafia network, and assistance was lent whenever it was needed.

There may, however, been one meeting which did take place which must be dealt with if we are to confront all of the evidence that exists to suggest a conspiracy with high-level participation, and that is a meeting that took place at the home of Texas oilman Clint Murchison on the night before the assassination, and which, if true, would implicate Lyndon Johnson in the conspiracy to kill the man he would replace. But before we confront that event, we need to fill in the gaps, as best one can, in the events – or at least in the contours of events – which took place after Lee Oswald returned from Mexico City. And unfortunately, the source which has provided such rich detail about the circumstances of Oswald's stay in New Orleans, Judyth Baker, frankly admits that she had only intermittent telephone contact with Oswald and David Ferrie in the lead-up to the assassination itself.

Oswald told Baker, as we have seen, that after the failed attempt to deliver the "product" to a contact in Mexico City, he'd been assigned to keeping tabs on a group of right-wing extremists ("nuts") who were planning the assassination of the President. Baker is certain that Oswald admired and respected JFK – in fact, she says that Lee turned her around with respect to her assessment of Kennedy – and Oswald's commitment to keeping watch over a group determined to murder him was a logical extension of the rationale he, along with David Ferrie and Mary Sherman, had used for their work on the cancer bioweapon they hoped would kill Castro and reduce the anti-Castro Cubans' taste for revenge over JFK's perceived wrongs. But at the same time, Oswald had had concerns going back to New Orleans that he might be being set up as a patsy for the crime when it was committed. Moreover, he feared that if he fled his family might be harmed in retaliation. So he soldiered on.

However, there is evidence that Oswald did more than simply continue on the path he was assigned – no doubt by David Phillips. The President was scheduled to make a visit to Chicago to watch the Army-Navy football game on November 2, but on October 30, the FBI received a warning from an informant named "Lee" that an assassination attempt would be made by several shooters with high powered rifles from office buildings[38] as JFK made his way to the game through downtown Chicago. The FBI refused to act, saying this was the Secret Service's jurisdiction, and subsequently an arrest was made of a former Marine who had the hallmarks of being set up, as was Oswald, to be a patsy in the event the assassination attempt was successful. JFK's trip was canceled at the last minute; the reason given to the press – some of whom had already departed Washington on the press plane – was that the turmoil created by the

---

[38] This is the very phrasing used by Joseph Milteer in an FBI surveillance recording (https://www.youtube.com/watch?v=EdbVyhzCcq4) about an attempt that would be made in Miami – and which prompted the cancellation of a motorcade planned for JFK's November 19 Miami trip. Perhaps tellingly, the change to the route of his Dallas motorcade to include the sharp – and deadly – turn from Houston onto Elm was also approved on this day.

coup against Ngo Dinh Diem in South Vietnam and Diem's assassination. Though there were corroborating reports of shooter teams readying for Kennedy's arrival and surveillance of them took place, with some even taken into custody, no formal charges were ever placed, nor were the identities of any of them – save Thomas Valee, the alleged patsy – ever revealed. Secret Service agents were warned never to speak of the Chicago plot, and when the ARRB requested files relating to the episode on the plot, the Secret Service illegally destroyed all relevant documents.[39]

Judyth Baker says that Oswald had told her that Mary Sherman, who was no doubt frustrated and disappointed by the failure of The Project to assuage the anger of the anti-Castro Cubans, and who had extensive contacts in Chicago, continued to work with Lee after his return from Mexico City and provided Oswald with contacts in Chicago. (Sherman herself would come to a violent end days before she was scheduled to testify before the Warren Commission.[40]) Moreover, both Baker and Marina Oswald believe

[39] The best account of the Chicago plot is in Douglass (2008); the destruction of the relevant documents is recounted in Horne's *Inside the Assassination Record Review Board* (Self-published in 5 vols, 2009). The Milteer story is told at length by ex-FBI agent Don Adams in *From an Office Building with a High-powered Rifle* (Walterville: Trine Day, 2012).

that Lee's connections with certain – though not all – FBI agents

allowed him to transmit this warning, possibly along with another

which is alleged to have been sent to all FBI offices in the early

hours of November 17, alerting bureau offices of a likely

assassination attempt by a right-wing militant group in Dallas on

November 22. This message disappeared from office files soon after

the assassination, and a copy of it was only obtained by researcher

Mark Lane under the Freedom of Information Act in 1976.

As the day of JFK's trip to Dallas grew nearer, Baker says

that Oswald became more and more alarmed that the assassination

was going ahead as planned *and* that he had been identified as "the

fall guy" who would be framed to take the blame for the President's

murder. Baker, herself riveted with fear – and with a packed

suitcase under her bed in anticipation of them both fleeing, as

planned, to Latin America – begged Oswald to escape the net of the

conspirators while he could, but he reiterated his belief that to do so

would put his family at serious risk of retribution.[41] He added,

---

[40] Her story is told in Haslam's *Dr. Mary's Monkey* (Walterville: Trine Day, 2014).

[41] It's worth noting here that a government agency like the CIA might not be expected to engage in retribution for its own sake. The Mafia, however, made revenge killings part of their code of honor, and the fact that Oswald was linked to

""They'd just get another gun to take my place . . . If I stay, that will be one less bullet aimed at Kennedy."[42]

This remark, made in their last phone conversation (made at 11 PM, Dallas time, November 20, only 36 hours before the assassination) is important for two reasons. One, it implies that Oswald would, as part of his covert activities to infiltrate, "keep an eye on" and eventually try to thwart the conspiracy, act as one of the shooters in Dealey Plaza. And second, it implies that the conspirators assumed Oswald's involvement, making it that much easier for them to make the assassination the work of a "lone nut." We'll return to this fact further on. Moreover, in that same conversation Oswald told Baker that "he was no longer alone, and an abort team had been called in to help him. 'Even though they're going to try to kill him,' he said, 'I've sent out information that might be able to save him.'" This, too, will become important further on; an abort team seems to have been present in Dealey Plaza, but to have failed its mission.

---

the Mafia, both by his own connections and those of his uncle, made it that much more likely that, were he to walk away from his involvement in a mob-sanctioned hit, his family could be made to pay the price.

[42] Near the end of that conversation, Oswald also said, in response to Baker's desperation at what was unfolding, "Stop it! I can still do something. Maybe I can fire a warning shot." Baker, p. 519.

We know very little more about Oswald's activities in the days immediately before the assassination. We do know that on Thursday, after work, he uncharacteristically asked a co-worker at the TSBD for a ride to Irving, where Marina was living with Ruth Paine, that he spent the night there and that when he left for work in the morning he left his wedding ring in a cup on Marina's dresser and his wallet, containing nearly two hundred dollars, in her drawer. He then rode to the TSBD with the co-worker carrying a long package wrapped in brown. This has repeatedly and wrongly been taken as an indication that he was carrying a rifle, but the dimensions of the package, tucked under his armpit as it was, make it clear that, even broken down, neither the Mannlicher Carcano nor the Mauser which was first reported to have been found could have been in the package.

There are two other events worth noting in the 24 hours before the assassination, both of them having taken place on the evening of the 21st. The first involves the activities of a significant number of agents from the President's Secret Service detachment partying until the early hours of the morning (beyond 3 AM) at a bar in Ft. Worth owned by a friend of Jack Ruby, and in the company of strippers from Ruby's Carousel Club in Dallas, a short drive away. In the last decade or two, we have learned enough to have discarded the spit and polish, ramrod-straight image of the Secret Service, but this kind of behavior on the part of agents expected to be at their best for an assignment that would begin in only a few hours is telling. Moreover, the reaction time of the agents in the follow-up car in Dealey Plaza that day would be repeatedly criticized – including remarks made by the Warren Commission – and one can only wonder at the intersection of a blatant violation of the Secret Service code, the involvement of associates of Jack Ruby and the subsequent assassination of the President.

But far more dramatic, and controversial, are events that have come to light mostly by way of Madeleine Brown, purportedly Lyndon Johnson's mistress.[43] She alleges that she attended a dinner party at the Dallas home of Clint Murchison, a wealthy Texas oilman, also attended by H.L. Hunt, J. Edgar Hoover, Richard Nixon and, later, LBJ himself. The power figures at the party retreated to another room after LBJ's arrival, and after meeting for a half hour,

---

[43] Brown's story appears in her *Texas in the Morning* (Baltimore: Conservatory Press, 1997).

LBJ emerged, very agitated, and said to her as he left, "After tomorrow, those goddamn Kennedys will never embarrass me again. That's no threat. That's a promise." Weeks later, on New Year's Eve of 1963, Brown says she asked Johnson directly whether or not he had been responsible for JFK's death. Johnson became angry and replied, "Texas oil and ... renegade intelligence bastards in Washington" had been responsible.

Brown's claims have never been proven, nor definitely disproven. Richard Nixon was, indeed, in the Dallas Ft. Worth area until the morning of the assassination. Curiously, he could not remember how he heard of JFK's death, changing his story several times. More important, perhaps, is the testimony of two members of Murchison's household staff which confirms that such a party, with such a formidable guest list, did take place.[44] What is significant about Brown's story, however, is that it suggests what may be the most plausible characterization of Johnson's place in the events *leading up to* the assassination: that he was the passive recipient of

---

[44] There is an account of Brown's story, and the witnesses who confirm the party took place, in Nigel Turner's *History Channel* series, "The Men Who Killed Kennedy," Part 9. The episode was suppressed after a lawsuit by Johnson's family.

benefits from the murder, that he may have had advance knowledge that the attempt would be made in Dallas, but that he neither initiated, participated in – nor, probably, attempted to put a stop to – the conspiracy to kill his predecessor. What his role may have been in the cover-up of the assassination we will examine later.

V

Dealey Plaza

In the case of the assassination itself, we have almost the reverse of the situation faced in so many other aspects of the conspiracy: an overabundance of evidentiary material. More than a hundred people were gathered in and around the Plaza that day, giving us a wealth of testimony – some of it contradictory, some of it complementary – but no indisputable blueprint for assembling the parts of the puzzle.

This simple fact makes it easy for any discussion to get lost in the myriad details of what witnesses say they heard, what they saw, and what the film and acoustic record seems to tell us. And, given that such once-unassailable touchstones as the Zapruder film have been demonstrated to be unreliable as empirical records of what happened,[45] one can be tempted to throw up one's hands at the prospect of developing a satisfactory overview of event.

---

[45] Douglas Horne's analysis of the problems with the Zapruder film's handling, and the likelihood that it was transported to a lab in New York and altered on Saturday, is probably the most thorough.

But there is one indisputable study of one important event in the sequence that can stand as a kind of landmark from which other details can be plotted and fleshed out, Sherry Fiester's *Enemy of the Truth*.[46] Fiester is a retired crime scene investigator who for years resisted her sister's urging that she do a professional assessment of the evidence of what took place in Dealey Plaza, Fiester assuming that it must have already been done, probably many times. When she learned that *a thorough CSI report by a qualified professional had never been done*, she was stunned and set out to do one herself.[47] Fiester's book is so thoroughly professional, and so carefully explains in exhaustive detail all the things that must go into a CSI report and why, it can at times be daunting for the non-professional. However, it is one of the two or three studies to have appeared in recent years that demonstrates both the highest degree of attention to the science of ballistics and conclusions that are supported by that science. Fiester demonstrates conclusively – on a variety of bases –

---

[46] Southlake: JFK Lancer, 2012.

[47] Throughout the history of official reports on the assassination, one of the most glaring flaws has been the degree to which professional crime investigators have rarely, if ever been part of the overall direction of an investigation. Lawyers, political officials and congressional staffers have dominated throughout – some of them honest brokers and hard workers, no doubt, but not professionally qualified to do a forensic investigation.

that the single bullet theory is the impossibility that researchers have maintained it was almost from the beginning of the controversy over the Warren Commission's findings.[48] But Fiester surprised everyone, Warren commission defenders and critics alike, by demonstrating that the shot which struck JFK in the head, driving his head "back and to the left" as the courtroom mantra of Stone's *JFK* puts it, actually came, not from the Grassy Knoll immediately north and west of Elm St., but from the South Knoll (or from the top of the bridge) at the far end of the Triple Underpass.

The strength of this conclusion is actually rather apparent to anyone who has toured Dealey Plaza and noted that the curve of Elm St. once it passes the TBSD actually points traffic towards the South Knoll while it follows the bend to the left, then straightens out once it reaches the underpass. Moreover, Fiester demonstrates that all of the forensics – head wound mechanics, fracture sequencing of skulls, blood spatter pattern analysis and more – confirm that the fatal head shot came from the area of the South Knoll. More startling still is

---

[48] Here again, the single bullet theory was introduced by Arlen Spector, not a qualified forensic investigator, to explain away gross anomalies that appeared in the lone gunman/three-shot narrative.

the fact that there was a witness who reported shots coming from that direction, Robert Plumlee.

Robert "Tosh" Plumlee was a contract pilot for the CIA beginning in the mid-1950s. He flew clandestine flights running arms to Castro in Cuba before Castro came to power, and after the government turned against Castro, he was assigned to the JM/WAVE station from which anti-Castro activities were conducted. Plumlee says that on November 20 he was assigned as a copilot on a secret flight from south Florida to Dallas, with stops along the way to pick up passengers in Tampa and New Orleans, and that when they were underway, his pilot, with whom he had worked previously, explained that they were transporting an abort team to Dallas to prevent an attempt on the President's life. Weather delayed them once they reached the Dallas area on the 22nd, but when they finally arrived, as members of the team went in various directions, the pilot asked Plumlee if he'd like to go along to Dealey Plaza as a spotter.

When they arrived, they took up positions on the south side of the plaza, but Plumlee says that they were late, there was disorganization and bad radio contact among the members of the team, and the motorcade arrived before they could position themselves. As the President's car started down Elm, Plumlee heard 4-5 shots and said that at least one came from behind him and to his left: the parking lot behind the picket fence at the top of the South Knoll. Seeing the President obviously mortally wounded, he and the pilot ran to the top of the knoll and down the other side to escape, the pilot slipping on the down side in mud from the morning rain. They stopped in a parking lot on their way back to the airport so the pilot could change, then transported as many members of the team as they could wait for back to Florida.[49] Plumlee said that on the return trip the members of the team were somber, which he took to be a sign they had failed their mission – making him permanently unable to entertain an obvious possibility: that he had been assigned to transport the assassination team to the site under the guise of transporting an abort team. Had they been the assassination team, he felt, they would have been excited on the return trip.

There are some wrinkles in Plumlee's story that require us to interpret it, rather than to accept it simply at face value.

Oswald's mention to Judyth Baker that an abort team "had been called in to help" him took place in their conversation of November 20th – the day Plumlee said he got his assignment. However, there is no guarantee that either Oswald or Plumlee – or even Plumlee's pilot – were told the truth. We have to keep in mind, first of all, the "need to know" *modus operandi* of the intelligence services: Plumlee did not need to know whom he was transporting, nor did he ask; he was filled in by a man – a handler – who had given an explanation, but the explanation may have been partial – or the handler may have deliberately misinformed Plumlee. Oswald himself was, at this point, no doubt still an operative of his David Phillips/Maurice Bishop handler, and it is likely Phillips/Bishop was the person to whom Lee turned for "help."[50] Phillips/Bishop might easily have conned Oswald with a false promise of help in order to keep him in place to "take the fall."

---

[50] It's also possible that Oswald's suspicions that he would be used as a patsy for the assassination led him to use other channels to get help – perhaps the same channels he may have used to alert the FBI of the Chicago plot. But even if the team Plumlee helped transport was truly an abort team, it doesn't negate the possibility of CIA involvement the assassination plot itself: the need-to-know basis upon which things were done leads inevitably to compartmentalization, in which case the left hand may be working directly at cross-purposes with the right.

As important is another wrinkle in Plumlee's story that seems to contradict other things we know. Plumlee said that one of the people on the team was a man he had known from other operations, but only as "Colonel Rawlston." Years later, he was to discover that "the Colonel" was Johnny Roselli, a Miami Mafia chief, former manager of a Havana casino owned by the mob, and a Mafia boss with whom the CIA had developed a relationship with regard to the killing of Fidel Castro. Given those credentials, one would expect Roselli to be on the side of the conspirators that day in Dallas, not part of an abort team – unless, of course, Roselli was acting as a double-agent: were there a CIA contingent that was actually trying to prevent the assassination, it's possible that Roselli was working in concert with it, rather than with the Phillips/Bishop contingent. But there's more.

James Files, at the time a low-level driver for Mafia hit-man Chuck Nicoletti, has claimed that, after the failure of the Chicago plot, he was ordered by Nicoletti to transport weapons to Dallas for a subsequent attempt. On the morning of the assassination, Files said, Roselli – who claimed he had arrived on a "military flight" – spoke to Nicoletti of there being an abort team and wanting to pull out of the operation. According to Files, Nicoletti recruited him on the spot to replace Roselli and told Files to position himself on the Grassy Knoll and to take a shot only if it appeared others had missed and Kennedy would escape the plaza alive; Nicoletti would fire from the DalTex building across the street from the TSBD. Files claims that he fired the shot that struck the President in the head.[51]

There are enough accuracies and irregularities in Files' story to suggest that he was in Dealey Plaza on that day, that he was part of the plot, but that he was not a shooter. Since an operation of the kind most likely performed in this case would almost certainly have a spotter/radio man accompanying each shooter, it's possible that Files (who says he was completely alone on the Knoll, in contradiction to almost all eyewitness testimony) was acting in that capacity and embellished on the real story to put himself at the center of it. However, his mention of Roselli and an abort team coincides with Plumlee's account, though it does not clarify why Roselli would have flown in with the abort team – unless he was concealing from Nicoletti that he was part of a contingent genuinely trying to abort the assassination and, playing a double role, Roselli

---

[51] Files' story is recounted in Jim Maars, *op.cit*, pp. 294-97.

had pretended to be working in concert with Nicoletti and other

Phillips/Bishop operatives (Files claims he was in touch with

Phillips and Oswald both when he first arrived in Dallas), and used

the story of the abort team as a subterfuge to explain his decision to

be absent when the shooting started.[52]

Whether or not there was an actual abort team or this was

merely a ploy invented to keep Oswald handy for the fall is not

relevant to our purposes. But there is one other post-assassination

claim that is worth factoring into our calculations for the fleshing out

of one part of the story. Chauncy Holt, who died in 1997, claimed

that he worked as an accountant for the mobster Meyer Lansky, but

that he also forged documents for clandestine CIA operations. Holt

says that he had produced false Secret Service credentials for

operatives who would be in Dealey Plaza and that he was one of the

"three tramps" who were arrested but were later unaccounted for,

giving rise to the suspicion that they were part of the plot.

---

[52] In 1975 Roselli told columnist Jack Anderson that Jack Ruby was "one of our boys" and had killed Oswald on orders to silence him. Roselli also agreed to testify before the HSCA, but before he could do so "he was found garroted, stabbed and dismembered, floating in an oil drum off the coast of Florida." (Benson, p. 388)

In later years, there were claims that others had been identified as the tramps, but there are inconsistencies in the alternative story that is proposed.[53] However, there have always been stories, often ignored by the Warren Commission or fundamentally changed in the commission's account, of individuals – particularly near the Grassy Knoll – showing Secret Service identification badges and ordering people away from the area; in several cases, film was confiscated from bystanders and never returned. However, records show that no Secret Service personnel had been posted in the plaza that day. Those who were there were part of the detachments protecting JFK and Lyndon Johnson, were in the respective follow-up cars, and went to the Parkland hospital with the motorcade; none were left behind, let alone were there any there in advance of the motorcade's arrival to direct bystanders away from the Grassy Knoll before the shooting began.

Theorizing about the number of shooters, their positions and, now, even their identities, has continued apace virtually from the moment the first shots were fired, since people in different parts of the plaza recall different numbers of shots, different sequencing and

[53] Maars, *op.cit.*, recounts all the stories.

differing directions from which the shooting seemed to originated. A clear preference for the Grassy Knoll as being the likely spot for one shooter or team developed immediately as those standing along Elm Street charged up the knoll in response to their certainty that they had heard shots from there, or seen either flashes or smoke emanating from there. Even several Dallas policemen made that estimation. But in the parking lot behind the picket fence, alleged Secret Service agents waved the crowd and the police off, saying they had the situation under control.

Others were convinced that shots came from behind, in the direction of either the TSBD or the DalTex building. Indeed, the famous Altgens photo which shows a wide angle of JFK's car and Elm Street as his hands seem to reach for his throat shows several of the (real) agents in the follow-up car turning towards the rear at the sound of the first shot or shots, though both Ken O'Donnell and Dave Powers, in the same car with the agents, felt shots had come from in front of the President's car. And, of course, there is Fiester's virtually unassailable analysis.

Rather than focusing on actual locations, perhaps it's best to remember that triangulation always offers the best opportunity, or set of opportunities, to stage an assassination, and that is all but certain to have been the case in Dallas that day. If we take Fiester's identification of the South Knoll as one position, the Grassy Knoll – based on multiple witnesses' testimonies – as another, and a rear position that would be needed to account for both JFK's back wound, as well as John Connolly's wounds, and the bullet which seems to have ricocheted off the pavement and a fragment from it struck James Tague in the cheek under the Triple Underpass, then we have at least three positions. However, given that at least three shots had to have come from behind, it is entirely possible that there were two rearward positions: those most frequently cited are one of the lower floors of the DalTex Building and the TSBD – though the latter would have been from a different position than the so-called "sniper's nest" proposed by the Warren Commission.[54]

Calculating teams of two, we are probably looking at a total of 6-8 shooters and spotters. In addition, there is likely to have been one strategically placed observer/controller to issue commencement

---

[54] The "sniper's nest" would have been ideal for a shot up Houston Street, before JFK's car made the turn onto Elm – one of the many reasons suggesting a lone shooter would never have passed up the opportunity to take that shot. But taking a shot that early would eliminate the possibility of the triangulation that existed once the car turned onto Elm.

commands by radio and to signal the outcome of the attempt. Added to those +/- nine persons, we must imagine 5-7, or even as many as 10 individuals in the plaza posing as Secret Service agents, perhaps posing as onlookers and available to help – even to deliver a *coup de gras*, if necessary. So the number of personnel in the entire team was likely to be twenty or more.[55]

Where was Lee Oswald during all this? We don't entirely know. He was seen eating his lunch in the TSBD lunchroom minutes before the motorcade arrived; he was seen drinking a coke by a Dallas policeman moments after the shooting in virtually the same area; and there has been ongoing controversy about whether someone standing in the doorway of the TSBD in the Altgens photo is Oswald or a co-worker named Billy Lovelady. Given what we have been able to reconstruct of Oswald's personality, his ability to exercise great *sang froid* in times of stress and his hope in what he might be able to accomplish that day – all gleaned from Judyth

---

[55] The number of wounds President Kennedy suffered is still unclear and a matter of reasonable, if not entirely measured, disagreement among researchers. Undoubtedly there was at least one shot to the back, one to the throat and one to the head. But it's also possible that there were other shots to the head, the evidence of which were disguised or obliterated either accidentally, by subsequent shots, or deliberately during the autopsy at Bethesda.

Baker's account – I think we can speculate that he was relieved of any actual participation in the shooting that morning. Though his comments to Baker in their last conversation ("one less bullet for Kennedy"; "fire a warning shot") suggest he thought he would have a rifle available to him at the critical moment, he was likely put in some kind of "stand-by" mode by Phillips/Bishop, or by someone acting with his authority. Thus it would make sense that Oswald went to eat his lunch as though nothing out of the ordinary were going on, idled down to the entrance to see the limousine go by, and then returned to the lunchroom to take a moment, absorb the fact that he'd failed entirely in what he'd set out to do and decide what his next move should be.

After doing so, Oswald seems to have moved quickly but calmly to what was probably a prearranged plan of action. He made his way back to his room, changed his shirt, grabbed his pistol (one suspects because he realized he might be walking into a trap) and made his way to a pre-assigned location to meet his handler or a "cut-out." It seems likely that, perhaps unaware of the role he was playing, Dallas police officer J.D. Tippet stopped outside Oswald's home and gave a signal with a horn honk – most probably just an indication that things were to proceed as planned. Soon after, it's likely that Tippett was ambushed and murdered, perhaps as part of the plan to frame Oswald, while Lee made his way to the Texas Theater. There, he seems to have tried sitting next to a number of people, as though looking for a contact he wouldn't necessarily recognize. When police arrived in numbers and with speed completely inappropriate to someone entering a movie theater without paying, Oswald started to try to fight his way out, then gave up the effort. His fate was sealed.

VI

From Parkland to Bethesda

In the first days after Lee Oswald was murdered by Jack Ruby

in the basement of the Dallas police headquarters, a joke went round

saying that the Dallas police were changing their name to the

Keystone Cops – Max Sennet's silent film-era group of bumbling

but lovable law enforcement officers. Though there might have been

some justification in the comparison, the truth may have been much darker, as we'll see in another section. But one unfortunate effect of the general impression that Dallas was a place in which plodding, good-enough-for-government-work standards prevailed was the carryover effect that impression had on the public's view of Parkland Hospital, its staff, and especially the observations which were made by the doctors who treated JFK in his dying moments.

When the Warren Commission encountered the differences between the observations recorded by the dozen or so physicians in attendance in Trauma 1 at Parkland and the report prepared by the three autopsy doctors at Bethesda some eight hours later – differences that were so dramatic as to allow one to imagine the two groups had observed different bodies – the Warren Commission summarily dismissed the Parkland doctors' observations as mistaken. In the days before the public had learned to suspect the competence, the veracity, or both of the Warren Commission's investigation, it was not difficult to transfer one's impressions of the sloppy, "hick" police force onto the Parkland staff, thinking them country doctors who were blind-sided by events, and to credit the Bethesda team – military doctors at the country's premier naval hospital – with accuracy, efficiency and truthfulness in their work.

Sadly, it was the doctors at Parkland who should have been credited with objective, professional comportment; since the truth began to come out, there were many who felt that the Bethesda autopsy team should have been charged, with criminal negligence and fraud.

When the President arrived at the hospital, between 5 and 8 minutes after the shooting, he was taken to Trauma 1 in the Emergency section of the hospital. Charles Baxter was in charge of Emergency; he would later develop the Parkland Formula for fluid resuscitation with burn victims, one of the first treatments for burns that recognized the importance of rehydration and management of electrolytes – a measure of Baxter's and the hospital's competence at the time. There was little that could be done. Even Jacqueline Kennedy, sitting in the limousine as agent Clint Hill tried to pry her husband loose from her arms, said, "You know he's dead. Leave me alone." The team of doctors in Trauma 1 took standard measures, including a tracheostomy, for treating a patient with massive gunshot wounds – which, it should be noted, are common in emergency rooms in urban hospitals – but within a short period of time it was clear there was no way to revive the President's vital signs, and at 1 PM he was pronounced dead.

The actions taken by the doctors in Trauma 1 at Parkland have never been questioned: they did as much as anyone could have; no one could have saved the President – even today. What has been at issue is what the doctors *saw*. But it is important to underline the fact that their observations, both written and remembered, were at issue only because they conflicted with – indeed, contradicted – the Bethesda autopsy report. While an autopsy might be expected to provide a more reliable record of such things as wounds, whether or not they were of entry or exit and at what angle they entered and exited, it is worth noting, for example, that Dr. Malcolm Perry, the surgeon who performed the tracheostomy on the President at Parkland "was experienced with gunshot wounds, having treated between one hundred fifty to two hundred gunshot victims."[56] He called the throat wound observed by all the attending physicians, and through which he cut a small incision to insert the breathing tube, "a wound of entry."[57] In that the Bethesda team *did not even note a*

---

[56] Fiester, p. 271.

[57] Under pressure from the Secret Service, Perry backed off his description somewhat, acknowledging that it could have been an exit wound. However, every medical professional at Parkland who observed it described it as an entry wound. Perry maintains today that it was an entry wound, though he will not go on the record saying so.

throat wound until word of Perry's description on Saturday morning *after the autopsy had been completed*, one is hardly led to have confidence in the autopsy report.[58]

More to the point are the descriptions of the President's head wounds that were witnessed by the Parkland doctors – and, importantly, one nurse who had treated numerous gunshot wounds suffered in deer hunting accidents and caused by high powered rifles. With reference to the major head wound, Anthony Summers says,

> Seventeen of the medical staff who observed the President in
>
> Dallas were to describe the massive defect as having been
>
> more at the *back* of the head than
>
> at the side . . . The only neurosurgeon present at the President's
>
> deathbed, Dr.
>
> Kemp Clark, described the wound as a 'large, gaping loss of
>
> tissue' located
>
> at the 'back of the head . . . toward the right side'." [59]

---

[58] It must be said, at least somewhat in the autopsy team's defense, that a jagged tear in the President's throat several times the size of a tracheostomy incision was visible by the time the body arrived at Bethesda, virtually obliterating the throat wound of entry *and* the incision.

[59] Summers, *Not in Your Lifetime: The Assassination of* JFK (London: Headline

Dr. Robert McClelland, who took his position at the head of the President, saw that "the right posterior portion of the skull had been blasted . . . some of the cerebellar tissue had been blasted out." Elsewhere, Dr. McClellan has described seeing cerebellar tissue falling out of the wound; the cerebellum consists of unique, very recognizable tissue and is located virtually *beneath* the brain proper, at the top of the spinal column.

There have been attempts to ascribe the Parkland physicians' observations to natural haste in the course of trying to save a dying patient, but these hardly warrant response: emergency room physicians are trained to *observe as much as they possibly can* about a patient's condition precisely because, in emergency situations, gathering information is critical. Moreover, to ascribe the virtually identical observations of eighteen trained medical personnel to mistakes and oversight is to propose that eighteen people experienced a simultaneous hallucination: mistakes and oversights take place randomly, not with uniformity; eighteen identical observations point towards authenticity, not error. And, in fact, many who had visual exposure to the President's body at *Bethesda* concur with the medical staff's observations: they include two x-ray technicians, an autopsy assistant and two FBI agents who took notes during the autopsy.[60]

It is quite clear that the Parkland doctors' observations were accurate, and they are important because *a 'blow-out' wound described by everyone at Parkland could only be an exit wound, the projectile which caused the damage could only have entered from the front – in Fiester's analysis, from the South Knoll – and the single assassin conclusion in the Warren Commission holds no water.*[61] In other words, the observations of the Parkland Hospital staff are entirely consistent with what would be expected from the narrative we have seen up until now: the preparation by experienced intelligence operatives of a professional assassination, designed for maximum firepower from hidden triangulated positions in a setting

---

[60] Even Clint Hill, who covered the President and Mrs. Kennedy with his body on the trip from the plaza to Parkland, and two other agents supported the staff's observations, Hill saying that "the right rear portion of his [the President's] head was missing."

[61] We've ignored completely a wealth of other evidence gathered by researchers over the years demonstrating, for instance, that the so-called "magic bullet" theory could be true only in violation of the laws of physics, that the Mannlicher-Carcano was incapable of being fired in the fashion the Warren Commission describes, and that the description, composition and weight of bullets and bullet fragments found do not support the commission's conclusions.

designed to produce maximum confusion and easy egress for the teams of assassins.

Had the letter of the law been observed at Parkland Hospital, there might have been at least a chance of the full extent of the President's actual wounds having been made public.[62] Texas law required that an autopsy of a murder victim take place in the locale in which the murder had taken place. While it may have seemed understandable at the time that Mrs. Kennedy and the Secret Service would have preferred an autopsy in the nation's capitol under military supervision, tempers flared almost violently – guns were drawn by the Secret Service – when the county coroner tried to enforce the law and prevent the President's body from being removed from Parkland for the trip back to Love Field and, eventually, Washington. The fact that the efforts of local officials quickly and understandably wilted in the face of the weapons of the Secret Service started the sequence of events that, were we not already talking about the only assassination of an American

---

[62] This may also reflect wishful thinking: no doubt the conspiracy had contingency plans in the event of a Dallas autopsy.

president in modern times, might be the most bizarre and improbable – not to mention treasonous – chapter in this sad story.

Though the events surrounding the President's body in the subsequent 12 to 14 hours seem so beyond the pale – and at times even macabre – as to be unbelievable, it seems best to present them, not as alternatives to any official version, but as a simple narrative of what we know must have happened. As Stone's *JFK* has Jim Garrison say to his unbelieving staff as they grasp the dimensions of the plot he feels they've stumbled upon, "We're through the looking-glass here, people." And indeed we are.

But at the same time, we are also on some of the firmest ground researchers have established in the more than half century since the assassination. For, along with the work of Fiester, the most unflinchingly thorough, systematic and irrefutable research into the assassination – most of it, like Fiester's, empirically-based – has been done on the Bethesda autopsy: first David Lifton's 1982 *Best Evidence*,[63] and then Douglas Horne's 5-volume *tour de force*, *Inside the Assassination Records Review Board*, which takes

---

[63] New York: Macmillan, 1980

Lifton's findings and builds a truly admirable and complex edifice of empirical investigative reasoning.

However, operating "through the looking glass" can require different kinds of navigation than we are accustomed to in the more familiar and at least somewhat predictable world of the everyday. Most especially, one must avoid the temptation to jump to conclusions, to assume the worst or to imagine that, since the seemingly impossible now seems possible or even certain, that the impossible is always the right answer to a question. This is particularly true when we look at the question of motivations as they apply to events subsequent to the shooting.

There are those who believe that the entirety of the assassination plot, from its inception to its execution to its aftermath was orchestrated by a Ludlum-like cabal which has taken control of the US government – that has been in control since time immemorial, some would say – and that everything that took place was done at the behest of the cabal. I do not take that view. I do not exclude it as a possibility, but I consider it remote. As has been said already, the plot to assassinate John Kennedy was devised and undertaken by a relatively select group of self-appointed arbiters of the direction American policy would take in the second half of the 20th century, radical elements from the intelligence community, the military, the Mafia and anti-Castro Cubans who saw JFK's death as a key to achieving their individual and mutual goals. But these individuals did not control the entirety of the governmental mechanisms that would be needed to carry out the cover-up of what actually happened in Dealey Plaza. And therein lies the rub.

In order to imagine, and to accept, that such widely-placed individuals as the Secret Service detachment aboard Air Force One as it returned to Washington, the autopsy team at Bethesda, and the Chief Justice of the United States, Earl Warren – a liberal who was publically vilified by the very right wing forces behind the assassination – took part in a cover-up, one needs to find a motive powerful enough and wide-reaching enough to provoke the widespread falsification of documents, events and even testimony that took place after the fact of John Kennedy's murder. And that motive exists.

Earl Warren refused, when first approached on November 29 by Nicholas Katzenbach and Archibald Cox, to chair the commission Lyndon Johnson intended to appoint to investigate the assassination.

However, he was immediately summoned to the White House and given what some call "the Johnson treatment" of alternating plea and harangue, and subsequently accepted the job. High on the list of reasons Johnson gave were the chaos that could spread through the country if a full account of the events were not given. But woven within that message was the clear implication that, were there evidence that the assassination had been engineered by Fidel Castro, the public outcry could lead to World War III and the deaths of millions. Warren left the meeting with tears in his eyes.

Whether Johnson was the instigator of the assassination (I think this not very likely), a "silent partner" in the conspiracy (possible, but not yet sufficiently proven), or merely an "informed beneficiary" (the most likely case), one could imagine that the upper level conspirators – above even the likes of David Phillips – had prepared and begun to disseminate the logic behind the marching orders Johnson gave Warren, and that the construction of a plausible alternative to what had happened – or what may have happened – was high in the minds of those involved in events immediately subsequent to the assassination. This need not have been an act of complicity to murder on their part: on the contrary, they might well have seen their actions as in the best interests of the entire country's security – an easy leap to make in those days only thirteen months removed from the moment when we all thought a nuclear exchange might erupt in the 1962 Cuban Crisis.

We don't know who may have participated in the cover-up because they were part of the assassination conspiracy, knowing accessories after the fact or simply dupes of a convenient cover story that – much in the tradition of intelligence agencies everywhere – recruited the efforts of others by pretending to cover up an entirely different story than the one they were actually hiding. The American people should have had access to the truth, whatever it was. But knowing that there may have been other, less malignant motives for cooperating in a cover-up may help some make their way through a landscape that takes on mind-boggling proportions as we move through the hours immediately after the President's murder.

And, indeed, we have to confront almost immediately a likely scenario that is hard to digest. For it appears that, after the Dallas coffin provided by the O'Neal funeral home was loaded onto Air Force One, and most probably during the swearing in of Lyndon Johnson, when everyone was gathered in one part of the aircraft, the

President's body was removed from the coffin, place in a zippered body bag – from which witnesses at Bethesda clearly remember him being removed – and most likely placed in a storage hold forward and below, near the cockpit area.

At first glance, this may seem incomprehensible: a fallen leader's body unceremoniously transferred from an expensive casket to a body bag and placed in a storage compartment like a piece of baggage. However, if we keep in mind that the Secret Service had, only fifteen minutes earlier, pushed the Dallas county medical examiner against a wall with guns drawn and in violation of Texas law had made off with the coffin containing the President's body, we can see that there is every reason to assume that agents feared the Dallas police might arrive in force at any moment and refuse to allow the plane to take off. Hiding the body – however ineffective that might actually have been – could easily have seemed the only measure to defend against that possibility.[64]

---

[64] I have presented the moving of the President's body in the light of less malevolent motives. There is a school of thought which says that members of the Secret Service may have been involved with more malevolent motives, may even have been party to some parts of the assassination. This is an entirely plausible interpretation, but is as yet unproven.

Whatever the case, Doug Horne's exhaustive analysis of arrival times both at Andrews Air Force Base and at the Bethesda hospital, of eyewitnesses, and of records demonstrates that the President's body arrived at the rear loading dock of Bethesda in a plain shipping casket as much as 45 minutes before the Navy ambulance which held the Dallas casket, Mrs. Kennedy and Robert Kennedy arrived at the front of the hospital. So confused were things that an honor guard assigned to escort the President's body wandered frantically around the hospital grounds for nearly a half hour before linking up with the Dallas casket – which was empty – and escorting it into the building.

Numerous witnesses have testified to seeing the shipping casket arrive at the rear loading dock, and many were also privy to the casket's opening and the removal of a standard, zippered body bag containing the President's body.[65] Moreover, others testify to seeing the President's body removed from a decorative coffin like the Dallas coffin. Horne pieces together the time line to show that there were two separate groups of witnesses to these events, and that

---

[65] At the suggestion of one of the nurses at Parkland, the President's body, still exuding fluids, was wrapped in a plastic mattress cover before being placed in the Dallas coffin provided by O'Neal's.

there was ample time in between them to allow for the President's body to be transferred back into the Dallas coffin before it was again removed from the coffin in front of the second audience.[66]

Once again, we must ask a simple question: why? What could have been the purpose of this macabre game of musical coffins, differing arrival times, different removals of the President's body before different audiences? The answer to this question was first posed by Robert Lifton in *Best Evidence*, and later dramatically augmented by Horne's work. Then a graduate student in engineering at UCLA, Lifton had been troubled by inconsistencies in the Warren Report and engaged regularly with one of the commission lawyers, Wesley J. Liebeler, himself by then a law professor at UCLA, about them. He was received bemusedly and politely with his questions and challenges until one day he presented Liebeler with a quote from the notes of the two FBI agents present at the autopsy in which they said that, on the removal and examination of the body, Dr. Humes, who led the autopsy, noted "a tracheotomy

---

[66] There are also differences in the background to autopsy photos that betray they were taken in different locations.

had been performed as well as surgery of the head area, namely, in the top of the skull."[67]

Liebeler immediately recognized that this was evidence that had slipped by the commission staff and was a game-changer, for there was no "surgery of the head area" performed at Parkland, nor should there have been any opportunity for such surgery to take place subsequently, since the President's body was thought to have remained in the Dallas coffin throughout the flight to Andrews and the ambulance trip from Andrews to Bethesda. Liebeler found this evidence so shocking that, a complete supporter of the commission's report until that time, he immediately sent out a letter to members of the commission's staff explaining what Lifton had found and saying that the investigation had to be reopened.

Liebeler's letter was to no avail. However, Lifton, and Horne after him, pursued the mention of head surgery and demonstrated conclusively that the frontal damage shown in autopsy photographs and x-rays was not present at Parkland, that a surgical saw had been used to create the appearance of frontal damage *and* to obscure the entry wound Parkland staff had seen,[68] and discovered anomalies in

[67] Lifton, *op. cit.*, p.172.

the autopsy photos and the x-rays that indicated extensive

falsification and the probable destruction of considerable numbers of

each. It's quite clear as well that, for instance, Humes and his

colleagues completed the autopsy without having identified the

throat wound described as an entry wound by the Parkland doctors,

partly because it had by the time of their examination become the

long, jagged tear visible on some of the autopsy photos. He only

learned of the wound after communication with the Parkland doctors

by phone, and he did not exact enough information from them – or

did not *want* to exact enough information from them – to be able to

identify the radical alteration and enlargement of the tracheostomy

incision – which the Parkland doctors said was very small and had

sealed itself upon removal of the tube.[69] The revelation of the throat

wound on Saturday morning forced Humes to write a completely

new autopsy report and to, incredibly, burn his autopsy notes.[70]

---

[68] Malcolm MacDuff, the acting press secretary, had pointed to his head when he announced the President's death and described the fatal wound, indicating exactly the position the Parkland staff described as one of the entry wounds.

[69] It's worth noting here that none of the three-member autopsy team at Bethesda were experienced at forensic pathology, let alone gunshot wounds, and two of them had been acting as upper-level administrators for years, not performing autopsies.

[70] Humes claimed the notes had the President's blood smeared on them and he did not want them to become some kind of collector's item.

The autopsy had other troubling aspects – many of which, it has been noted, would have made it inadmissible as evidence in any court proceeding. There were two examinations of the brain which took place on two separate occasions, days apart; two of the team members were present at one, and all three at the other. However, the third member was unaware until years later that the first examination had taken place, and the procedures reported to have taken place in the first would have sufficiently destroyed enough brain tissue to make the second – which the third doctor reported took place on a pristine specimen – impossible. Moreover, during the autopsy there were regular interruptions in the procedures by people in the gallery, some in military uniforms, some civilians. The interruptions were sufficient for Humes, who should have been directing the autopsy, to ask in exasperation, "Who's in charge here?" – to which one of the civilians responded tersely, "I am."

Lifton's groundbreaking discoveries, greatly amplified and augmented by Horne's relentless pursuit of both evidence and the way in which the parts of the puzzle fit together make it clear that, indeed, John Kennedy's body was clandestinely handled in various ways and by various means in the twelve or so hours immediately after his death, and the evidence was manipulated and revised – and in some cases, destroyed – over the coming weeks and months. Again, we have to ask why – or, more specifically, to what ends?

In this case, it is hard to imagine that, for instance, Humes and his colleagues were part of the plot directed by David Phillips. In fact, Humes has been described repeatedly as someone who "goes along to get along," a career officer who wanted nothing more than to move successfully to upper ranks and, finally, a comfortable retirement. But he was also a military officer who had to obey orders; and he had all the hallmarks, in his comportment at the autopsy, his clumsy attempt to change aspects of the autopsy, and in his nervous and often clumsy obfuscation in giving testimony – to the Warren Commission, the HSCA and the ARRB – of someone who was being directed from above, as did the other colleague who seems to have been in on some aspect of the "fix," Navy Dr. Thornton Boswell. One could easily imagine them succumbing to the same pressures as Earl Warren did in the name of national security.

More perplexing, and still to be resolved, is the question of the moving of the President's body and the surgery/damage done to both his head wound[71] and his throat. Horne feels that someone in the Secret Service must have had foreknowledge – in the capacity of accomplice(s) – to the assassination, and his suspicions fall on Roy Kellerman, who was riding "shotgun" in the presidential limousine and who seemed to direct everything that happened in the movement of the President's body at Parkland and on Air Force One. Vince Palamara has done a great deal of work uncovering, not only gross shortcomings in the way the Secret Service protected the President in Dallas, but sentiments expressed by some members of the Secret Service during Kennedy's short tenure that indicated unhappiness with his politics. But there is not conclusive evidence that allows us to point a definitive finger at overt complicity by the members of the Secret Service.

There is, however, no doubt that the President's body, the autopsy itself, the autopsy photographs and x-rays and the autopsy report were either mishandled or dramatically altered to support what would become "the lone assassin" theory. And there can be little doubt that the creation of a patsy by the conspirators, and the

---

[71] Lifton and Horne both demonstrate that the surgery was not confined to skull bone, but included brain tissue as well.

mounting of a quiet, perhaps completely covert, but nonetheless effective campaign to have him convicted in the press, would have influenced even those who, perhaps unwittingly in some cases, went along with the program. It would be a long time before the real events surrounding the autopsy began to be revealed, and it would certainly be too late, by years, to save Lee Oswald.

VII

Death, the Silencer

Only moments after Secret Service agents – no doubt

coincidentally – pulled their weapons, pushed the county medical

examiner against the wall and spirited the President's body away to

Love Field, Lee Oswald arrived at the Dallas City Hall and, at about

the time the Dallas casket was loaded onto Air Force One, Oswald

was booked. Though he would spend the next 48 hours in police

custody, it is remarkable how little we know of what he said during

that time. There was no audio recording of his interrogation, and,

even though he was characterized early on by NBC as the prime suspect in the assassination, there was no stenographer present during any of the interrogations that weekend.

By the time of the formal ending of the autopsy in Bethesda,[72] Oswald would learn from newsmen during his brief encounter with the press that he had been charged with the shooting of the President and his face would reveal the look of frustration we've already noted. But perhaps as important was an incident that occurred moments later, when the Dallas district attorney, Henry Wade, was taking random questions from shouting reporters. Asked about connections with communist or other groups, Wade remarks that Oswald was a member of "the Free Cuba Movement, or whatever." Wade is immediately corrected and told it was the Fair Play for Cuba Movement. The person who corrected him was Jack Ruby.

The Dallas night club owner had been seen in Parkland hospital that afternoon – had, indeed, spoken with a national news reporter, Seth Cantor, whom he had known when Cantor had worked in Dallas, at about the time of the announcement of the President's death. Later, he was seen and photographed at the Dallas police

---

[72] The time of the end of the formal autopsy has been reported as midnight on the 22nd, but there is evidence that procedures continued to be carried out after that time.

headquarters, he had brought a dozen sandwiches for police during the evening, and he had even tried once to walk into the office where Oswald was being interrogated. The Warren Commission mostly ignored or dismissed these reports and sightings, simply saying in the case of Cantor's testimony that he was probably mistaken. Researchers have noted each one of the sightings and speculated on their significance – the unexplained fascination with the case Ruby seemed to have, for instance, and the ease with which he moved in and out of the Dallas police headquarters – but the one thing that should stand out to anyone who looks at these accounts dispassionately is the question of why a Dallas night club owner, on the evening of the assassination, would know of and bother to (rightly) correct the information given by a district attorney about the alleged suspect's activities *in New Orleans*.

Judyth Baker has recounted a May episode at David Ferrie's apartment, early in her involvement with The Project, during which a man named "Sparky" Rubenstein appeared, was introduced to her, and even gave her money when he heard about how she had been cheated by her first landlady in New Orleans at a place Lee had installed her – he said, at Sparky's suggestion. In the course of the conversation, Sparky referred to having known Lee since he was a child, largely through his connections with Lee's Uncle Dutz and Carlos Marcello. When Baker asked if Sparky knew about the lab, Ferrie said that he "brings money to help finance it."

That evening they all, along with several other apparent mobsters, were wined and dined, and Sparky gave Lee and Judyth the car he was driving – which Carlos Marcello had loaned him – for the balance of the evening. She saw Sparky one more time, in early June, when they were all taken to the famous 500 Club and Lee spent some time at Marcello's table with Sparky and a man Baker was told was Clay Shaw; Oswald later explained that they had been discussing arms shipments to Venezuela. Because she had always known the man as "Sparky," and had been too much in shock to peruse pictures of Jack Ruby after she saw Lee shot on live television, it was only in 1999, after she had emerged from her self-imposed exile, that Baker learned that Marcello's colleague, "Sparky", and Ruby were the same person.

In fact, Ruby's connections to organized crime extended back to his youth. He was purportedly a runner for Al Capone in his teens, was a small-time operative for the Chicago mob, and had

moved to Dallas at their behest to manage their gambling interests.[73]
Most especially, Ruby had been involved in anti-Castro activities as
part of the mob's attempts to regain the lucrative racketeering
"property" it had been for them before Castro's revolution. Though
we know too little about the Mafia's organization – a tangled web
woven to deceive almost as dense and convoluted as that of the
intelligence community – to be able to say definitively who did what
in any aspect of the organization's activities, it is probably not
overstating the case to say that Ruby was at the center of the mob's
involvement in the assassination, perhaps even its "point man."

The sightings of Ruby during the immediate run-up to and
aftermath of the assassination and his behavior during those days
suggest him having some kind of role. In addition to the Parkland
and Dallas police headquarters sightings, Ruby was seen at about 11
AM on the day of the assassination driving a green pickup truck
stopped by the side of the rode on Elm Street just before the triple
underpass dropping off someone carrying a long, wrapped package.
Ruby appeared intent on being seen in various offices during the

---

[73] There is also evidence that he did work for Richard Nixon when Nixon was a
junior congressman. Summers has a good overview of Ruby/Rubenstein's mob
activities, pp. 401-406.

hour before and just after the assassination, and in the assassination aftermath he was observed showing what seemed to be feigned grief and concern over the President's death and – the concern he claims led him to murder Oswald – the sorrow he felt for the President's widow. However, knowing what we know about the Mafia, its code of honor and his role as a mid-level, and probably expendable, mob operative, the emotional turbulence that seems to have gripped Ruby during that weekend most certainly had other causes.

We don't know enough to be able to say what the exact plan for Oswald's framing might have been, but one can be fairly certain that, if there was strong-arm activity to be conducted, that would have fallen easily into the brief of mob members who had agreed to the hit. It's possible that Oswald was meant to have been shot in the TSBD and the murder made to appear as a suicide – a *modus operandi* that seems to have been engaged in a number of the suspicious deaths associated with the assassination that occurred in the coming years. It's possible that there should have been a shoot-out between Oswald and J.D. Tippet. And there may have been other plans – probably several of which could be engaged if others failed. What is certain is that, while he may have been a patsy, Oswald was not a dupe.

He saw what was coming and repeated his growing concern about how he would be used in his conversations with Judyth Baker. And the fact that he retrieved his pistol in the visit he made to his room after the assassination, but before his arrest, makes clear he wasn't going to let himself take a fall if he could help it. It's entirely possible that he thought he was dealing with two different CIA (and/or FBI) factions in his activities, one which was planning the assassination, and the other allowing him to think they were against it and could help him thwart it. When he thought his mission had failed, Oswald might well have abandoned the plan he had agreed to with the people he thought were part of the pro-assassination faction and been trying to contact those he thought were opposed to it.

Whatever the case, he had been taken alive and, given all he knew, he had to be silenced. It's entirely possible that Ruby's repeated visits to police headquarters on Friday and Saturday – most especially including the attempt to walk in on Oswald's interrogation – were tentative sorties made in the hope he could slip in and do his job: he admitted that he was carrying his .38 revolver during these visits, then later retracted the statement when he realized it could be used to prove premeditation at his murder trial. But it's also likely that he felt great ambivalence: he had been chosen, probably partly because of his expendability, partly because of his reputation for violence (the nick-name "Sparky" had been given to him because of his flaring temper), by the upper-echelon of the mob to silence a witness who knew far too much; he was undoubtedly promised money and help in his defense if he succeeded and violence done to his family if he refused. But this was a friend, one he had known since the young man was a child.

So it's not surprising to learn that, on two different occasions, calls were made to the Dallas police on Saturday by someone with "a white, male voice" warning that an attempt on Oswald's life would be made during the transfer of the suspect the short distance to the county jail. One of those who received the call thought the voice familiar, and later recognized it as having been that of Ruby. Perhaps desperately, but certainly naively, Ruby probably hoped he could stave off the inevitable. But, in the end, he did his duty and, likely aided by some members of the Dallas police who helped him gain entry through an unguarded stairwell with an unlocked door, committed what someone has called "the first murder committed on live television." Poignantly, as others wrestled Ruby away, one of the police officers accompanying Oswald leaned down to him as he lay on the garage floor and told him the wound looked bad, asking if there was anything he wanted to say. Oswald paused, then gave a tight shake of his head. Any chance of the man who knew close to the complete story of the assassination speaking about it died with his determination to maintain the code of silence – if only for the few minutes he had left to live.

Of course, Lee Oswald was not the last fatality to occur as a consequence of the events in Dallas. The improbably high distribution of non-natural deaths among witnesses to the Kennedy assassination in the years since it took place has become almost a mantra delivered by those who set out to convince disbelievers in a conspiracy. Various calculations have been made,[74] but whether one finds them persuasive or not,[75] the deaths themselves are often notable for their mob-like style. Gunshots are common – and often

---

[74] One – among many – site which contains comparisons of various calculations is https://www.lewrockwell.com/2013/04/richard-charnin/the-mysterious-deaths-of-jfk-murder-witnesses/

[75] I do.

attributed to self-inflicted wounds despite the fact that, for instance, a wound was found on the left side of the head of a right-handed victim, or that the victim's family was convinced there was absolutely no reason for them to have taken their life. Strange assortments of alcohol and barbiturate poisoning, even when no prescription drugs seem to have been in the possession of the victim, abound. And then there are the blatant instances of gangland-style executions: the grisly death of Johnny Roselli shortly before he was to testify before HSCA topping the list.

Whatever the provenance of these deaths, one can easily imagine this being the role the mob had agreed to play in the aftermath of the virtual *coup d'etat* that took place in Dallas that day. Contract murders have been the stock-in-trade of gangsters since time immemorial, and the *vendetta* that was often attached to the contracts could be passed down from one generation to the next.[76] Judyth Baker – someone who certainly knew far more than anyone should have about the backdrop to the assassination – cites the deaths as the reason she chose to remain underground for decades,

---

[76] There is a wealth of research that suggests that Robert Kennedy was killed by the same powers that killed his brother. But that's another story.

and to this day she is cautious about divulging her whereabouts, one suspects wisely so.

But perhaps the most deeply ironic post-assassination death involved one of the principal actors from that weekend – the man who had carried out the first mob murder in the sequence, Jack Ruby himself. Ruby, according to what David Ferrie told Baker, was helping to funnel money into The Project while the attempt to create a cancer virus to kill Castro was underway. Ruby's original conviction for killing Oswald had been overturned in October of 1966, and he was awaiting retrial at a venue outside of Dallas as his lawyers had requested when, on November 9, he was taken to Parkland hospital with uncontrollable coughing and nausea. The doctors' diagnosis was pneumonia, but the following day they announced he had advanced cancer of the lungs. Within days they announced it was inoperable, and he died on January 3, 1967. He had told his jailers that a doctor who had visited him earlier had injected him with cancer cells – a story that was scoffed at by the media when it came out. But Ruby died 28 days after he was first diagnosed – exactly the number of days, Baker tells us, that passed between the injection of the prisoner at the Jackson State hospital and his death. Knowing what we know about The Project, the "product" and the blinding speed with which it seems to have coursed through Ruby's body, one cannot help but be reminded of the phrase, "galloping cancer."

VII

From the New Frontier to the Great Society

Late in September of 1964, then-President Lyndon Johnson visited Sacramento, where my family then lived, on what was an early campaign trip in the run-up to the November presidential election. My father wouldn't let me go to Johnson's appearance downtown at the state capitol: our aging Volkswagen had a bad backfire. But we were a former military family and had access to the Air Force base from which Johnson would depart, and my father felt comfortable letting me go to the sendoff there. And so it happened that, less than ten months after the assassination in Dallas, I found myself behind a rope line at the edge of a runway where Air Force One was parked when the open limousine in which Johnson was riding came by.

There was a good ten feet or more separating the rope line from the path of the limousine, but feeling this was a once-in-a-lifetime opportunity, I ducked under the rope and moved towards the car, which was flanked by Secret Servicemen, four on each side. The second of them made a motion with his arm to push me back as the President, his face showing he was obviously eager to press some flesh, reached in my direction. I ducked the man's movement and came up with my hand held out, not more than six inches from Johnson's. But before we could grasp one another's hands, the third Secret Serviceman slammed his forearm across my chest and sent me reeling back into the crowd as the limousine rolled past. When I told my father what had happened, he snorted, "They're not taking any chances these days."

It's strange to think back to that day, so soon after JFK's death, and so near to the edge of the long, slippery slope that would carry the country downhill for . . . well, for all of my youth and the better part of my lifetime. In a meeting with the Joint Chiefs of Staff shortly after he took office, Johnson had responded to their urgings on the question of military involvement by the US in Vietnam, "You get me elected and I'll give you your damned war."[77] Two and a half years later, I would see the guy who lived next door for the last time when we had our draft physicals together. I received a 1-Y deferment; he died the day after Christmas, 1969 in Quang Nam Province.

By the time Johnson was elected in '64, my father had joined the War on Poverty, working with Youth Opportunity Centers trying to find jobs for ghetto youths; but his admiration for Johnson would wane, then turn to deep disappointment as he saw the country he himself had fought for descend into flames and chaos, mindlessly killing its children on the battlefield – almost as a prelude to killing them on college campuses.

Hindsight isn't just 20/20, it can be 40/10.[78] There are those who seem to think – Oliver Stone and James Douglass, among them – the that JFK's death robbed us of an era of social justice and social change that would have brought the country into a new era, across a

---

[77] Stanley Karnow, *Vietnam: A History*, (New York: Penguin, 1997) p. 342. This quote appears in various accounts, with and without the "damned."
[78] Rated able to see at 40 feet what the average person can only see at 10.

New Frontier to become a truly great society. That may be. Certainly one can point to the death of Abraham Lincoln and the subsequent travesty that was Reconstruction and say that the death of one man changed history – perhaps for all time. But Abraham Lincoln would only have had four years to put in place the machinery that would have had to carry the country through decades of rebuilding, social as well as economic, if the defeat of slavery were to become the true democratization of America. JFK would only have had five in which to set the country on a path that would carry it through the decades necessary to eliminate racism once and for all, establish social justice as the bedrock of American life, cope with the siren song of consumer capitalism, and resist a military convinced of its mission to – in the words of Kennedy's own Secretary of Defense, but spoken on the watch of the new president – "enforce democracy around the world" – to name only the highlights of the challenges he would have faced.

However, one thing is clear: a Kennedy presidency through the years 1964 to 1969 would have afforded the country a period of true leadership – leadership that may only have been latent when JFK entered office, but which ripened and wizened immeasurably in the face of the trials, domestic and international, the 35th president had faced in his first, all too brief thousand days. Intelligence, dignity and commitment would have remained the hallmarks of those times, and there is at least a chance that they would have done so for the majority of the country, that the catastrophic divisions that came to the surface during those years might have been avoided and the unanimity of earlier times – now in the service of genuinely enlightened goals – maintained.

So one must be careful in examining the one question we have postponed until now, but which must be faced: was Lyndon Johnson a usurper – at worst, a Macbeth whose consuming appetite for power led his country into moral ruin, at best, a willing benefactor of the actions of power brokers who operated in a sphere even higher than the one he moved in?

Johnson's life in politics was, like that of almost any Texas politician of his time, less than saintly. Not only did he likely fix elections, there have been allegations that he had a hit-man, Mac Wallace, at his disposal and turned to him when necessary.[79] Moreover, it is clear that Johnson's less-than-savory past was about

---

[79] See note 23 above.

to return to haunt him – and, potentially, a 1964 Kennedy-Johnson ticket – in the guise of what became known as The Bobby Baker Affair. Baker, the Secretary of the Senate and a Johnson protégé, had been targeted by a Senate investigation in September of 1963 and had to resign his post; his ties to Johnson gave rise to strong sentiment that Johnson should be jettisoned from the ticket in 1964. Given that the Baker affair came on the heels of another scandal over bribery on the part of another Johnson friend and associate, Billy Sol Estes, JFK is purported to have told his secretary, days before the assassination, that his '64 running mate would "not be Lyndon."[80] After Johnson became president, the Senate dropped investigations related to him.

When asked by a friend why he had accepted when JFK offered him the vice presidential spot on the 1960 ticket, Johnson purportedly replied, "I'm a gamblin' man." Certainly the rumors that he would be dumped in '64 cannot have given him confidence about how much time he had left in which to win his bet. But was

---

[80] I well remember reading at the time of a mysterious death tied to the Estes affair in which a death attributed to wounds in the back inflicted by a bolt action .22 rifle was ruled a suicide – little realizing at the time how many of these kinds of deaths lay in the country's future.

he willing to commit murder and treason in order to redeem what he had stake at the table?

I doubt it. Johnson was an old school pol with a healthy dash of good ole' boy criminality, Southern style. But, at least outside of the wheeling and dealing world of politics, he was not a brave man. He might have, from time to time, availed himself of the services of a hit-man – Mac Wallace, or some other lackey – but I suspect that he would have only done so when cornered. And even though one could argue that he certainly seemed backed into a corner by the back-to-back Estes and Baker scandals, I doubt he was prepared to launch an entire conspiracy of the complexity of the one that killed JFK to attain his ends. He didn't – to use his own vernacular – have the *cojones*.

However, had he been aware of a conspiracy that would have given him full deniability *and* ended up with him in the Oval Office, I have no doubt he would have at least stood at arms length, waiting to see what might come of it. He might, at first hearing, have dismissed it as "fantasy stuff." But when he learned that – as was probably true – the likes of Allen Dulles were behind it, and that his neighbor, J. Edgar Hoover, was willing to turn a blind eye to it . . .

my guess is that he would have said approximately what Madeleine Brown claims he said at Guy Murchison's on the night before the assassination. Moreover, if, as Brown claims he said at New Year's after the assassination, Texas oil money was bankrolling the conspiracy, how much more convenient for everybody.[81]

In short, I think it is unlikely Johnson played any formative role in planning the assassination of his predecessor.[82] However, I think it highly likely that he knew what Madeleine Brown says he knew at about the time she says he knew it. What's more, there seems little doubt that he did everything in his power to push the lone assassin explanation – right down to calls to the Dallas police on the day after the assassination, saying of Lee Oswald, "You've got your man." His appointments to the Warren Commission – *especially* the head, recently fired by JFK himself, of the very

---

[81] It's worth noting that Richard Nixon, whom Brown claims was in the meeting at Murchison's, was central to the planning for the Bay of Pigs that took place during the close of the Eisenhower administration. Moreover, Nixon's Chief of Staff, Bob Haldeman, says in his memoirs that, during the Watergate investigation, when Nixon referred several times to the problems that might arise if "the Bay of Pigs thing" came out in the investigation, he was using code to refer to the involvement in Watergate of operatives who had been involved in the assassination of JFK.

[82] *The Men Who Killed Kennedy* contains a very persuasive account of allegations of Johnson's involvement which, if substantiated, might give the lie to what I've said here and make LBJ a prime collaborator in the conspiracy. But for now they remain only allegations.

organization Kennedy wanted to "splinter into a thousand pieces" – makes it clear that Johnson assumed as much control over the machinery of cover-up as he could, and no doubt had his own people in the field monitoring the progress of things.

But most importantly, Lyndon Johnson, though he did push through some of Kennedy's legislative agenda – particularly the Civil Rights Act of 1964 – and launched the country off on its first, and really only attempt to undo the ghastly miscarriage known as Reconstruction – ultimately changed America forever where JFK might have kept it on a course for a future that would have allowed it to realize its latent potential, even greatness. He helped nurture the discourse of disparagement and outright attack that came to characterize his last years as president, and which have echoed down to our own times, crating a cacophony of opinionation, hyperbole and demagoguery. He nurtured the very intelligence agencies Kennedy hoped to dismantle, and in the process laid the foundation for the gross violations of democratic institutions that we think of when we think of the Watergate Affair, but which really reach out to a vast array of activities that, in a truly democratic society, would be considered criminal, sometimes even treasonous.

Finally, by creating in five short years a horribly wounded and infected social order that could be manipulated and used by an even more unscrupulous political operator – Richard Nixon – Johnson lured Americans, in their weariness, their anger and their frustration, down the dangerous road toward welcoming someone who promised to "make it all right." Therein lies perhaps the most tragic and the most portentous legacy of Johnson's tenure as president. For it made possible the callow and self-serving rhetoric of the Reagan years, the rhetoric which changed the New Frontier into "Morning in America," but exchanged the rhetoric of "what you can do for your country" for the rhetoric of "looking out for #1." And, though few realized it at the time, it allowed the pursuit of the "Great Society" to be replaced by "greed is good."

Great Britain recovered from Chamberlain; Germany recovered from Hitler and Italy from Mussolini. But, perhaps because democracy's greatest asset – that things change slowly, by increments, rather than by fiat – is also, in the hands of opportunists and demagogues, its greatest weakness, we are, today, living in an era of political vulgarity almost unprecedented in our history. The insults, half-truths and outright lies that today pass for political discourse would have been treated as demented, demonic or worse in a 1964 election with a Kennedy-Sanford (as JFK intimated he favored) ticket. But they are the currency of our times, and they set in painful perspective what we lost that day on Dealey Plaza. We lost the opportunity to use the American talent for meeting challenges for genuinely enlightened purposes. We lost the chance to use that old, Calvinistic tendency to engage in self-criticism for higher good – devoting it instead to leering at the foibles of celebrities and the *faux-pas* of public figures. And we lost our vision.

We lost the ability to shoot for the stars which was always an exercise in overreach, but which, tempered with the wisdom that an existential encounter with nuclear Armageddon, might have led to judicious, sober attempts to reach out beyond the narrow sphere of our own individual lives.

There is no guarantee that those things would have reached their full fruition had John Kennedy lived. But there is every certainty that they will be far more difficult to attain – indeed, may already be out of our reach – because he died.

The sun beat down on the Texas town

In the place of that one Lone Star

To the tune of a band a most noble man

Rode along in an open car.

With him his wife, in the summer of their life

And Texas governor, John Connolly . . .

--unfinished poem, Dan Shanahan, Spring 1964

Printed in Great Britain
by Amazon